HOW TO BECOME AN
Employer
of
Choice

HOW TO BECOME AN
Employer of Choice

Roger E. Herman
and Joyce L. Gioia

Oakhill Press
Winchester, Virginia

10   9   8   7   6   5   4   3   2

Library of Congress Cataloging-in-Publication Data

Herman, Roger E., 1943–
    How to Become an Employer of Choice / Roger E. Herman and Joyce
    L. Gioia
      p. cm.
    Includes bibliographical references and index.
    ISBN 1-886939-35-7
    1. Personnel management. 2. Management. I. Gioia, Joyce L. (Joyce
    Leah), 1947– II. Title.
    HF5549 .H4175 2000
    658.3—dc21   00-21845

                                                         CIP

Oakhill Press
461 Layside Drive
Winchester, VA 22602
800-32-BOOKS
Printed in the United States of America

DEDICATION

We dedicate this work to our children, who will "deliberately" work for employers of choice during their careers. Our children are our legacy and we're delighted that they all eagerly continue learning and growing. Each of them will have a significant impact on the world, and we're proud of every one of them.

So, we salute and appreciate Joyce's daughters Belinda, Melissa, and Samantha. The same recognition goes to Roger's children Scott and Jennifer, with a special acknowledgment to Bruce and Jeff, whom Roger was privileged to parent during their growing years.

CONTENTS

Foreword

People are basically good. They want to do the right things. They want to be motivated and inspired. They want to take initiative and feel the excitement and exhilaration of being energized. They want to become a part of something great. People want to be recognized and rewarded for what they accomplish.

These concepts are not difficult to understand. They're not even difficult to provide for and accomplish. However, in spite of the simplicity and purity of these ideas, most employers don't have very high levels of sensitivity to their people. This condition is unfortunate, for today we live in an era in which these ideas are more important than ever before because of the increasing speed of business, the impact of change and technology, and the changing values of today's workers. Today's workers want more than just a job or just a paycheck.

Employers who, for decades, took their people for granted are now having a more difficult time hiring employees, keeping employees, and getting the best work from them. Legions of managers are stuck in the old ways of doing things. Autocratic management styles, reinforced for years, are still practiced in many organizations. Old-line management practices won't work anymore. People previously accepted that old style, and the culture that went with it. They had to; there were no other choices. Today's workers, though, have choices, not only in the labor market, but in the amount of discretionary energy they exert in their jobs. Employees increasingly choose to work where they can learn and grow, and enjoy their employment.

You can't get the best from employees today by lighting a fire *beneath* them; you need to find a way to light a fire *within* them.

Today's employees are looking for employment environments that will take them far beyond the mediocre, the mundane, the everyday. They are looking for workplaces that are radically different than those found in their parents' era. Today's workers choose to work for employers who are different—for employers who really care. They want enlightened leaders who explain where they're going . . . and why. Growth, meaningful work, involvement, fun, and opportunities to make a difference are more important today than money to most employees.

Employers, on the other hand, still need competent people to get the work done. They need people who will stay for a while. They need stability. In the competitive labor market, many employers have begun waving a flag proclaiming that they are employers of choice.

Of course! Everyone wants their company to be the choice place to work. However, the phrase has become hollow, because no one has defined precisely what being an Employer of Choice means, and no one has done anything to set standards or explain how to become an Employer of Choice.

Now Roger Herman and Joyce Gioia have brought this picture into focus. In a much-needed book, they define exactly what an Employer of Choice is, and, at the same time, provide a model to show us what to do to legitimately earn such recognition. Not every company can be an Employer of Choice, but by following the recommendations and advice in this guidebook, many more employers will achieve this coveted status.

Bob Nelson
President, Nelson Motivation Inc.
Author, *1001 Ways to Reward Employees,*
1001 Ways to Energize Employees, and
1001 Ways to Take Initiative at Work

DEFINITION

Employer of Choice (n) im- (ploi er \ev chois **1.** Any employer of any size in the public, private, or not-for-profit sector that attracts, optimizes, and holds top talent for long tenure . . . because the employees choose to be there. **2.** A phrase which has fallen into common usage to describe such an employer, usually used as a self-description for the purposes of differentiation to recruit workers.

WHAT DOES IT REALLY MEAN TO BE AN "EMPLOYER OF CHOICE"?

The phrase "Employer of Choice" is falling into common usage in a way not dissimilar to the use of the word "excellence" in the 1980s. Not every 80's-era company achieved the excellence they touted. Likewise, not every company in the coming decades will become an Employer of Choice. Companies that were not excellent are still around today; companies that don't become employers of choice will continue to do business. The quality of their success will be different, as will their vulnerability to failure.

In contrast, those organizations which do earn the right to be described as employers of choice will enjoy a higher level of performance, greater workforce stability, and a level of continuity that assures preservation of the knowledge base, customer loyalty, employee satisfaction, and stronger profits.

To us, Employer of Choice means that workers—employees and contractors—*choose* to work for that employer . . . *when presented with other choices of employment.* This choice, then, is a conscious decision—or series of decisions—made when joining an organization and when deciding to *stay* with that organization. This deliberate choice will then influence productivity, as employees choose to do what will make their employer more successful.

DEFINITION

MARKETPLACE ISSUES

More so now than ever before, today's workers have choices. Everyone has a range of choices of occupation, geographical location, industry, and work arrangements. Our strong economy, which economists tell us will last until at least the later part of the first decade of the 21st century, ensures that we'll continue to have an abundance of employment opportunities.

In this seller's market, workers will make clear decisions about where they will work, why, and for how long. While each of us will establish our own personal decision-making criteria based on the individual needs of our companies, research shows that we have a number of common issues that will influence our choices. The more employers understand these common issues, the more steps they can take to strengthen their positions as employers of choice.

Employers of choice—in other words, those able to attract, optimize, and retain top talent—will enjoy a substantial tactical advantage over their competitors. They will have the knowledge, experience, resiliency, and power to respond quickly to the marketplace, delivering what customers want more efficiently and more effectively than competitors plagued by nagging employee turnover. This strength will allow them to win more business and maintain high levels of customer service and loyalty.

Employers of choice will compete for employees with the same power base that allows them to achieve high levels of customer satisfaction. Workers seeking better employment will naturally gravitate toward high performing organizations with a reputation for workforce stability. Just as in the marketplace where "the rich get richer," employers who become employers of choice will continue to get stronger. In today's sharply competitive world, this dynamic means they'll often enjoy a greater market share and earn higher profits—at the expense of their competitors. This book can help employers stay ahead of their competition and not be left in the dust.

ACKNOWLEDGMENTS

Defining a term that's come into common usage, then refining its meaning with depth, has been an enjoyable experience. We've invested hours and hours talking with pioneers in changing culture—in changing the way organizations position themselves in the world of employment. On this journey, we found profound thinkers and strategists with a genuine sensitivity to workplace communities. And we've discovered the more shallow opportunists who are focused on public relations and image hype designed to produce more resumes to be sorted. People seeking the right position for themselves see through the hype, and so did we. The comparison motivated us even more to define Employer of Choice so sincere employers would have a guide through this jungle.

We can't effectively thank all the researchers, corporate spokespersons, human resource professionals, public relations specialists, and journalists who collaborated with us in the development of this book. There were so many, to try to list them would take a lot of space . . . and we'd still miss important contributors. You all know who you are; we've thanked you along the way. Thanks again!

Thanks to our colleagues in The Workforce Stability Institute and in the Institute of Management Consultants who provided valuable insight into what works and what doesn't. We appreciate their reviews of our writing and the refinements that moved us toward the book you're about to read.

Our operations team at The Herman Group was, as usual, supportive beyond description. When busy consultants and speakers attempt to think, create, and write, having a highly competent team of people to manage business details makes a tremendous difference! A big salute to Kimberly Bauer, Cynthia Boren, Mark Funkhouser, and Carol McKinney.

Our children were usually understanding when the call of the writing pulled us away from family concerns. Thanks, Samantha, Belinda, Jennifer, Melissa, and Scott for your tolerance.

A special thanks to Kyung Ko Kim, our next-door neighbor, who volunteered to spend a few more minutes on his tractor each week to mow our lawn in addition to his own. That time was valuable in helping us concentrate on the development of this book.

And a special thanks to Andrew Perry for his special style of editing and to Jennifer Herman for her critical reading of portions of the text.

WHY BECOME AN EMPLOYER OF CHOICE?

The phrase "Employer of Choice" has picked up a considerable amount of popularity lately, but most employers really don't understand the importance of becoming an Employer of Choice. The phrase is more than just a buzzword; it is representative of a whole new design of corporate culture. It means that people will choose to work for you. It means that people will choose to really dedicate themselves to your success. It means that people will choose to stay with you, even when they are being courted by recruiters from other employers—recruiters with exceptionally attractive inducements.

In the years ahead, workforce stability will be a company's competitive edge. In these turbulent times, exacerbated by a tight labor market, employers will be continually challenged to locate, attract, optimize, and retain the talent they need to serve their customers. The most successful employers will be those who legitimately inspire highly talented workers to join them and stay with them.

What, precisely, are the benefits of becoming an Employer of Choice?

MARKETING AND RECRUITING

As the company becomes more widely known as a good place to work, an Employer of Choice will find that recruiting will be considerably easier. People will even approach the company them-selves, inquiring about employment opportunities. This attrac-tiveness will save the organization considerable expense in mar-keting and recruiting to attract the people that it wants and needs.

Instead of employing an army of recruiters, Employers of Choice will concentrate on evaluating the fine people who choose to apply. Most applicants will be high caliber candidates, so the choices will be difficult for the employer. The objective will shift from just getting people to apply to choosing the best of the best.

OPTIMIZING PERFORMANCE

With higher quality people on board, productivity will become significantly higher. As the company is able to hire the kinds of people it really wants, it will be able to help workers achieve a higher level of performance more quickly and with a greater level of consistency.

With a higher caliber of worker—a worker who has longer expe-rience with the employer—tasks get done more quickly, more thor-oughly, and more accurately. People performing the work are more confident about what they're doing, so their time is used much more efficiently. Corporate leaders are able to venture into the un-charted waters of new venues knowing that they're supported by people who have a good foundation and are ready to perform.

CHOOSING TO WORK, CHOOSING TO STAY

People will choose to join an employer, and *may* also make a con-scious choice to stay. When people remain with the organization for a longer period of time, the higher level of continuity benefits the employer tremendously. People work better together when they know each other better. There's a higher level of comfort, and of trust. Long-term employees understand the processes, the suppliers, and the customers, and they become more efficient and effective in a team-centered environment.

Having made the choice to join the company—and to stay with it—people will feel better about working there because it is a sta-ble work environment. The place is familiar, the work is familiar, and the co-workers are familiar. Their needs are met; this is the place for them.

REDUCED TURNOVER, ENHANCED LOYALTY

Certainly, the happier the employees are, the less turnover there will be. This reduced turnover will have a positive effect on the bottom line as well as on the morale and dedication of every employee.

Higher levels of loyalty will result in stronger relationships and a greater dedication to the quality of performance, production, and service. This higher level of quality, as well as reducing re-work, scrap, and after-sale problems, will build profitability for the company and pride for the employees.

FINDING BETTER PEOPLE

A company that is an Employer of Choice will be more attractive to prospective employees. This attractiveness will also enable the company to attract a higher caliber of worker. Not only will the company have more applicants to choose from, but the overall quality of applicants will be significantly better than companies which are not recognized as Employers of Choice.

> Red Auerbach, famed sports figure who built the Boston Celtics dynasty and legacy, once said, "Loyalty is a two-way street." He knew that if he expected his players to be loyal to the Celtics that the Celtics had to be loyal to them. He had a reputation for treating players fairly. Red made sure that the top talent in the league was attracted to the Celtics. Players wanted to play for him and for the Celtics, because they knew he would value and appreciate them. Among basketball teams, the Boston Celtics franchise was certainly an Employer of Choice.[1]

Mediocre workers will intentionally choose not to apply to such an organization, justifiably fearing that their performance would not be acceptable. Higher quality employees seek companies where they can be highly productive, where they can feel a part of something special, and where they can engender and represent a high level of achievement as part of the organization. These star performers choose star corporations because *that's where they feel they belong.*

EFFICIENCY, EFFECTIVENESS . . . PROFITABILITY

The company's recruiting process will be much more productive and streamlined, because their reputation will enhance its ability to attract the people it needs. This process will also serve as a pre-employment screen that will actually *eliminate* the substandard applicants that the organization doesn't want to consider. The company's attractiveness to higher-caliber applicants will result in greater profitability, as well as greater efficiency and effectiveness in the recruiting and retention process. Since the company will be more attractive, the necessity of heavy marketing and promotion for recruitment will be diminished significantly. The cost per recruit will drop dramatically.

> Bill Gates, chairman of Microsoft, believes part of the reason that they are able to get the highest caliber employees is that creative software developers want to work with other creative people who are excellent in their field. Microsoft also offers an opportunity for these talented, creative types to see their efforts implemented in high-volume, low-priced products. These predispositions give Microsoft an advantage in the recruitment process.[2]

A WAITING LIST OF WILLING WORKERS

Research has reinforced what Gates believes, that highly talented employees want to work with similar co-workers. The presence of top-flight employees and managers will attract similar applicants to the organization. Employees appreciate their co-workers when they observe them expending the same high level of effort and energy to complete every job. As employees recognize their appreciation of their co-workers, they will be inspired to stay with the organization for a longer time. As a result, the company will be both more attractive to prospective employees, and more attractive to those employees who are choosing to stay with the organization.

One of the results of attracting and retaining high-level employees will be that a waiting list to join the organization will develop. This enviable situation will be dramatically different from those companies that are not recognized as Employers of Choice. Those less fortunate companies will be forced to continue to scramble for the meager assets in the pool of less desirable applicants.

LESS STRESS, MORE FUN

Employers of Choice have less stress and more fun. It's that simple. There will be less disruption in attendance, and there will be less disruption in the workflow when people who have chosen to join the company choose to stay there and choose to make the best of their relationship with the company and their co-workers.

Managers and supervisors will have a much easier time doing their jobs because they will not be working against resistance from employees who would rather not be there. Working with employees who are there *by choice* is a much more enjoyable experience. Managers and supervisors can focus more on coaching, teaching, and supporting than on managing, controlling, and disciplining. This shift of focus will enable employees to be much happier in their work, reducing turnover among supervisors, reducing difficulties in supervisory performance, and significantly enhancing the supervisors' value in the company's overall equation.

PLANNING FOR CONTINUITY

When a company is an Employer of Choice, it can easily plan ahead, forecast, and use corporate resources efficiently over a long period of time. The employer will enjoy a dependable human resource base—both in quantity and quality.

The company will also enjoy a continuous knowledge base. Knowledge will not leave with employees who depart on an all too-frequent basis. Low turnover will result in a higher level of corporate knowledge remaining within the organization, thereby building efficiency and effectiveness while at the same time reducing re-work, accidents, and confusion.

GREATER ATTRACTIVENESS TO INVESTORS

Employers of Choice will be more attractive to investors because they will be recognized for their stability and their ability to respond more quickly to market opportunities and fluctuations. Employers of Choice will be more financially healthy as a result of their stability, because millions of dollars will not be pouring into retraining existing employees and marketing to new hires.

Investors look for companies with a predictable future. The more predictable the future, the more positive the future, and the more attractive the companies are to investors. With a stable workforce, Employers of Choice will be able to attract more investment dollars, enabling them to thrive and place themselves in an even more competitive position. They can then focus on capturing an even more significant portion of their markets.

INCREASED ATTRACTIVENESS TO CUSTOMERS

Employers of Choice will be more attractive to customers as well. This attractiveness will be critical in a relationship-based environment. Customers like to deal with the same people on a long-term basis. This relationship continuity builds stronger bonds and gives the customers a greater sense of comfort, confidence, and security.

Employers of Choice will enjoy a reputation for reliability, because they will be able to respond more legitimately and consistently to the inquiries and expectations of their customers. Because more experienced employees understand their customers, they're able to take good care of them. Customers appreciate employees who know their services and merchandise.

GREATER EFFICIENCY IN CUSTOMER SERVICE

The long-term expertise enjoyed by Employers of Choice will enable them to do a significantly better job for their customers. Each employee will have a higher level of experience in product lines and in meeting the expectations of the cus-

Unisys, the multi-national giant, considers employee satisfaction one of the legs of a "three-legged stool." The other two are customer focus and financial performance/reputation. Each of the company's 33,000 employees received a bronze three-legged stool lapel pin to reinforce the company's commitment to the philosophy. Its numerous employee-centered initiatives have helped the company increase its pace of growth, as well as its financial performance. Unisys offers satellite work centers and a "virtual university," along with an "employee share incentive scheme." These and other special employee offerings have helped the company maintain a relatively low rate of employee turnover. Payback on their debt of $1 billion was achieved more than one year early. Can you imagine how the market took that news?[3]

tomers. The memories of customer relationships and customer preferences will enhance profits and customer satisfaction. This level of experience will be particularly important for those high-maintenance customers who expect special service for special orders and unusual needs they may require from time to time.

EXCITING ENVIRONMENTS— THE PLACE EMPLOYEES WILL *WANT* TO BE!

Employers of Choice will typically be growth-oriented, although some will be content to maintain their status quo. Those Employers of Choice who concentrate on growth and expansion will generate an excitement in their workplace that will continually stimulate the people who have chosen to be there. That very growth promises greater security for all workers as well as better opportunities for companies and their employees. The long-term health of any given organization will support that company's image in the marketplace—as an Employer of Choice—and will enable the company to continually attract both the workers and the customers they desire. As the company continues to grow, more promotional opportunities will be available to those who have chosen to be a part of this preferred employment environment.

Employers of Choice will clearly differentiate themselves from their competitors in the employment, customer, investor, and supplier environments. This contrast (or differentiation) will build a higher level of profitability, security, and future success.

We recently received our new membership cards from the American Automobile Association (AAA). For the first time, there was no expiration date shown on the card, so we were concerned that something had not been done properly in the processing of our renewal payment. By the time we were able to call the local AAA office to inquire, it was after business hours. We spoke with an Emergency Road Service dispatcher who was totally familiar with the new card system and was able to explain it to us very clearly. As we began to wonder aloud if the renewal payment had indeed been received, the gentleman looked at his computer screen and told us the date our payment had been posted. We now have an even greater comfort about doing business with AAA because this employee had answers. And the employee felt good about being able to give us those answers as well.

THE DOWNSIDE

There is a disadvantage to being an Employer of Choice. Other employers will know that you've been able to attract really good people. Your company will become a hunting ground for recruiters from other less fortunate employers. We have worked with a number of companies that employ super people, so we've observed this phenomenon first-hand. The good people—who gravitate to Employers of Choice—get calls from recruiters several times a week. But—and this addition is an important "but"—they brush off the advances from these head-hunters to stay where they are. They *choose* to stay where they are happy.

THE DECISION

Once you've made the smart choice—the decision to be an Employer of Choice—it's time to look more specifically, more concretely, at how to go about initiating the processes of change in your company. In fact, the first thing you'll need to look at is just that—your company. How does it operate? How does it behave in the community, and how is it perceived? What kinds of things can you do to make your company more attractive to potential employees in today's competitive market? What sorts of things have other companies done to affect these important changes? In the next chapter we'll examine these issues in detail, and we'll explore the ways and means at your disposal to make your company an Employer of Choice.

Notes

1. Alan M. Weber, "Best firms don't need employee loyalty," *USA Today*, July 22, 1998.
2. www.hr-resource.com, "Recruitment and Retention."
3. "Unisys' performance rocketing," *The Dominion*, December 14, 1998.

THE COMPANY

As people consider which employer they'll join next, or whether they'll stay with their current employer, they become interested in a number of aspects of the company itself. They tend to be concerned about the company's strength, reputation, location, and social consciousness. They want to know about the people who work there, the facilities, and the work environment. Astute applicants learn a lot about the company they join, and current employees become more aware of company policies and positions.

Employers of Choice offer prospective employees plenty of information about the company, as well as the people who are already on their team. They have a story to tell, and potential or current employees appreciate the value of that information and insight. A significant part of the decision to choose a company to work for is emotionally based; a person has to feel like they "fit" comfortably within the organization. People will do research, perhaps in some serious depth, to learn about prospective employers. Make it easier for them to discover answers to their questions and concerns, and you'll have a better chance of encouraging them to choose your opportunity.

CORPORATE STABILITY

Most applicants seek a company that is financially stable. They look for an organization that has a solid history, an organization where employees feel secure. Other applicants, those more adventurous and willing to take risks, may be more interested in unproven start-ups or companies that are struggling and need help. The important issue here, in either case, is to convey the true and honest position of the company. Misleading or false information will be discovered eventually, and valued employees are likely to quit.

Provide applicants with plenty of information. More is *always* better than less. Arm prospective employees with plenty of details so there are few questions. Buyers—choicemakers—are more comfortable when they feel they are being given enough information to make educated decisions. This information can be provided in a number of forms: copy/collateral on a web site, printed materials, audio, or videotapes. You might even consider a CD-ROM presentation, depending on how much you have to say and how sophisticated your applicants might be technologically.

A HISTORY LESSON

Tell your company's story—the history from the time the company was founded. Most companies have a great story to tell, perhaps based on an Horatio Alger sort of legend, or perhaps flowing from a proud spin-off from another organization. An understanding of the company's life-to-date, of its heritage, will be of interest to prospective employees. Explain the employer's strengths and how smart decisions were made during the company's growth which brought it to the fine position it is today. This kind of information-sharing shifts one's impression of the company from an impersonal entity to one with a life . . . like a living organism.

Demonstrating a solid history usually helps deliver the evidence that workers seek: that this organization has been around for a while and will be for years to come. You want people to think, *I*

> At Ericsson Corporation in Lynchburg, Virginia, new hires hear about the historic meeting that marked the beginning of the Winshare Team Program at the company. This meeting also marked the change of ownership from GE to Ericsson. Before that time, the workers heard "do as you are told," "don't make waves," and "just do what we're paying you to do—nothing more." One of the workers remarked, "For all those years, you paid me for my hands, when you could have had my mind." With this dramatic comment, Ericsson ushered in their new employee-centered culture that values employee suggestions.

can invest my time and energies here and not worry about the company falling apart around me. I can make a difference here. The company is strong enough to follow through on my ideas, and I will have a good place to stay if I want to. People want to associate with an employer that's successful, one that has its act together and one that can be depended upon to continue to thrive.

WHAT'S COMING NEXT?

Explore your company's future. Forward-looking applicants seek employers that have a clear idea of their future. They ask: *Where is the company going? How does the company expect to get there? How can I contribute to the achievement of that objective?* They want to see how they fit into the present—and future—picture. Show the company's direction, even if the future is not carefully planned. Many applicants are attracted to companies with a clear direction, even if the paths are not thoroughly mapped yet. They want to help create the future. If your situation is that you know where you're headed, but don't know exactly how you'll get there—explain these circumstances and clearly show applicants what the opportunities are—for the company and for each person involved.

It might be helpful to tell applicants something about the company's strategic planning process, particularly if they'll be involved in the effort. It's not necessary to reveal intricate detail here, and closely guarded aspects of corporate strategy should *not* be revealed to applicants. The idea is to give people a sense that serious thought is given to planning, that the company is knowledgeable about its present and future environment, resources, and designs.

Workers choosing to join or remain with an Employer of Choice are future-focused. They're looking out for their future. Help them see how their future can be positively interwoven with the company's future. Show them that they can achieve their dreams and goals by staying with an organization that's moving in a direction that will be congruent with their personal path.

It's important to note that some applicants may not yet have a clear sense of what they want in their own future. Ask questions to help them appreciate their alternatives, then show how working with your company will help them move their own careers forward. Human resource professionals report that applicants are asking aggressive questions about career advancement opportunities in initial interviews.

REPUTATION COUNTS

Your company's reputation will be quite influential in the decision-making process of future and current employees. Each of us is naturally concerned with our own personal reputation, and our personal reputation is unquestionably linked with the reputation of our employer. Let's look at the various aspects of corporate reputation, recognizing that judgments will be made based on what others think of us. Good public relations does make a difference.

How well-known is the company? Some applicants want to join organizations that are well-known and highly regarded in their community or their industry. They're looking at their next employment being a steppingstone along a career path of working for a number of companies. Recognizable and respected names on their resumes represent a strength for future opportunities.

As prospective employees research potential employers, they'll often use the Internet to gather information to use in their decision-making process. What will they find? Has your company generated positive media coverage? What comes up as Internet browsers, metacrawlers, and search engines look for your company's name? How much is on your web site, making it convenient for people to learn what others say about you?

INDUSTRY RECOGNITION

Is your company respected in its industry? How is it known in the industry? For the high quality of its products? For innovation? For intellectual strength? For playing a leadership role? For being a rock-solid part of the industry's foundation, a leader that everyone looks to? An upstart, seen as leading significant change in the industry? An emerging company with great potential for major accomplishments?

Are members of the company invited to speak at industry conferences? Are their preferred topics, as requested by meeting planners, focused on the culture of the company? Are the company's innovations, technological advances, notable achievements, or intellectual prowess of interest to colleagues?

When members of your organization attend industry events, do employees of other companies in the field approach them about job opportunities with your company? How do your people respond? Do they demonstrate their pride in working for you? People who work for Employers of Choice love to talk positively about their employers. They're obviously proud of and excited about their contribution and their success.

Provide guidance and support to enable your employees to follow through in their interactions with prospective employees. What does your company do, through exhibits, event sponsorship, leadership roles in conference management and programming to send a message of attractiveness? Work with your company's marketing professionals to ensure consistency and comprehensiveness in your message—reaching prospective employees as well as prospective customers.

If your organization, like so many others, participates in job fairs to attract quality applicants, you may already have handout literature that all employees can use. Perhaps there is a slide show or CD-ROM that's used to present the company and its opportunities. Recruiters may have question-and-answer sheets for distribution or for training that could be made available to everyone. Give all your team members answers and information so they can accurately and proudly talk about the company, its career potential, and why it's a great place to be.

> Southwest Airlines reinforces its reputation through numerous speeches delivered throughout the country by its vice president of people and its vice president of people development, among others. As they share what they've accomplished, and some of the methods they've used, they enhance the reputation and mystique of the company. Since they're out with people in their field or related fields, they are accessible to receive inquiries about employment. And, by their titles alone, both their internal and external customers can see the dedication the airline has to its people.

Is your company cited in trade publications? Do members of the organization submit articles for publication in journals, magazines, and newsletters that reach your industry? Encourage the kind of public exposure that defines your company and its work in a positive light.

> Challenger, Gray & Christmas, an outplacement firm, emphasizes public relations as a corporate strategy. As a result, the company is well-known and has a positive reputation. Through publicity, the company has positioned itself as a leader in its field. This strong positioning contributes to the company's bottom line as more corporations choose to do business with them because of their image as an industry leader.

Explore opportunities to get positive exposure in publications outside your field, especially in national news magazines that may be read by applicants or those who influence the applicants you want to attract. Remember that workers are now jumping from one career field to another. Advertising and editorial recognition builds the kind of reputation that encourages workers to choose to associate with the company.

To build a positive image among college juniors, seniors, and graduate students, arrange for positive news about your company to be published in college and university newspapers, magazines directed toward that demographic segment, and annuals that are targeted toward graduating students looking for jobs. The articles don't have to be braggadocios, touting how wonderful your company is. A more powerful approach might be to talk about the positive things your company does—in the community, for its employees, in its industry. The key is to have lots of prospective employees get the message that this organization is a good employer doing good things. Nice people. Positive vibes. This company is a good outfit to work for.

People like to work for companies whose products and services are well-known and easily recognized. It's better when the company's output helps people, rather than just being a commercial product.

COMMUNITY RECOGNITION

What's your reputation in your community? Is your company involved with the chamber of commerce and other organizations that take a leadership role in your community? Today's workers are increasingly concerned about the health of the community in which they live and work. They'd like to see their employer as a positive local force, helping to make the area a better place to be, a place to raise a family, to settle for a long time.

Some companies demonstrate their civic commitment through the active involvement of a few senior corporate leaders. Even greater strength comes from a broader involvement of employees at all levels. Corporate citizenship means more than just donating money to worthy causes. The real power comes when a large number of employees are engaged in civic and other volunteer activities.

Your community probably has an abundance of service organizations that could benefit from funding, in-kind donations, and volunteer time from your company. Some examples are the Boy Scouts and Girl Scouts, Red Cross, chambers of commerce, Corporate Challenge, community celebrations, Jaycees, Meals on Wheels, and Habitat for Humanity.

An increasing number of companies are giving employees paid time off to work on civic and volunteer activities. There are multiple benefits from this strategy. First, the community is well-served and your company gains a reputation for being a good corporate citizen. This reputation enhances your image as an Employer of Choice. Second, participating employees feel good about the contribution they and their employer are making. In most cases, they quickly see how they're making a difference. This progress feels good. Third, employees working together with other volunteers learn leadership skills that can

> The corporate culture of Wal-Mart includes the commitment that each store is to be an integral and supportive part of the community in which it is located. Local charities are supported by the use of store resources and Wal-Mart people actively involved. Home Depot provides building materials and people for Habitat for Humanity home building projects.

> The employees of Bank of America participate in Team Bank of America's Volunteer Network, a program that's sponsored by the company. Through this program, employees have opportunities to engage in a variety of volunteer activities that make a difference. Some of the worthwhile pursuits include restoring homes for senior citizens, fund raising for charities, helping at homeless shelters, and cleaning up the

environment. Team leaders learn skills such as conflict resolution, speaking, and networking. Because they're working side by side with senior managers from other divisions, when they take the initiative, they garner attention. Some team leaders have been promoted at the bank as a result of their demonstration of leadership abilities in the volunteer setting.[1]

be applied on the job.

When disaster strikes, communities need a huge amount of resources quickly. People, equipment, organizational systems, space, and much more is needed. Contact city and county officials where your company is located and offer your assistance in advance. They'll probably be delighted to add everything you can offer to their databank of resources. If your company is spared when the tornado, flood, hurricane, earthquake, or other disaster strikes, your contribution of people, equipment, and expertise will be a blessing. Recognition—internally and externally—of your firm's commitment promotes and confirms your Employer of Choice positioning. You care about the community in which you live. See chapter 9 for a more in-depth discussion about employers making a difference in their communities.

Your Employer of Choice reputation can be enhanced by having an active speakers' bureau of employees who speak at meetings of local organizations such as the Rotary, the Kiwanis, the Business and Professional Women, Sertoma, the Ruritan, and the Exchange Club. Look for opportunities to provide speakers or subject matter for school functions, including teaching and mentoring roles—directly and through groups such as Junior Achievement. This kind of outreach delivers a positive, personal involvement of the employer in the community, and also provides a vehicle for employees to make a contribution to society.

WORTHY PRODUCTS AND SERVICES

People prefer to work for a company that produces goods and services that have an inherent positive value for society. Examples of such employers are manufacturers and distributors of pharmaceuticals, medical supplies, educational materials, food, and clothing.

Educators and other government employees stay in their jobs because they are delivering a value to society. Even though they could probably get paid more in the private sector, the opportunity to be of service to others every day draws and holds them in their positions. Firefighters, law enforcement officers, paramedics, hospital personnel, clergy, and social workers are more examples of people who are happy to stay in their lower-paying jobs because of the other "compensation" they receive doing their worthwhile work.

THE QUALITY ISSUE

Considerable emphasis has been placed on quality in recent years—concerns about quality of manufacture and quality of service lead the way. Workers want to see clear evidence of quality in the company they choose. They're looking for more than just a bunch of words and a nice campaign saying how wonderful quality is. The proof is in the performance. Does quality really have a genuine emphasis in the organization?

Employers of Choice demonstrate commitment to quality in design and manufacturing. Policies and procedures clearly state the rationale, expectations and methods of achieving high quality.

Quality in service to customers is desired more today than every before. We've always wanted decent service, but that attribute is highly valued today. People—in their business and personal lives—are moving at a frenetic pace. They have little patience for inadequate service. A pledge to deliver high quality service to customers—internal and external—is a characteristic of an Employer of Choice.

A commitment to quality in service for employees sends a very important message. Truly and demonstrably caring about employees and the issues that are important to them is practically a requirement of attaining recognition as an Employer of Choice.

> Varian Oncology Systems, Palo Alto, California, enjoys a very low turnover. Even though the company is nestled in Silicon Valley, where employers all around them are hungry for technologists, people tend to stay with Varian for a long time. The company's work is developing radiological therapy systems to reduce or eliminate cancer. Every employee there is dedicated to this highly meaningful work. People who work for the company see themselves on a mission to help wipe out a disease that kills thousands of people whose lives may be saved by their efforts.

Included in service to employees are such things as providing fast response to benefits claims, keeping records current, issuing identification cards (and replacements) quickly, and promptly answering employee questions about things that concern them.

As more employees work from home, from customer locations, from remote sites, and in virtual mode, more employee calls will come from the outside. Employers of Choice will assure that these calls are answered within three rings and that callers will be treated as if they were the company's best customers. Truck drivers and others who work through dispatchers at their companies often complain that they're treated like second-class citizens. Employees outside your physical environment should be treated especially well, since they don't usually enjoy the benefits of being inside with the rest of the team.

Companies that produce products with a reputation for high quality earn higher levels of respect from prospective and current employees. Even employees who have left your company will remember your emphasis on quality, and may be inspired to return to again associate with high quality performance. We'll see more boomerang employees—people who have left and want to come back—in the coming years, so maintaining the levels of quality people have come to expect is essential.

Rarely have we found a company worthy of being described as an Employer of Choice that has not placed a great deal of importance—of value—on high quality performance, goods and services, and the quality of care of its own people. The kind of company we're talking about concentrates on doing the right thing—all the time—in the best way possible. It's simply the way of life at an Employer of Choice.

SOCIAL CONSCIOUSNESS

There's a rising tide of social consciousness—among employees as well as employers. It's a sort of ethical belief in "doing the right thing." As people choose to do what they believe as the right thing, they're attracted to employers who articulate and demonstrate the same kind of beliefs.

Many employers attracted people with similar values when they supported the ban on doing business with South Africa during the apartheid years. Other employers gained respect when they voluntarily recalled products that had defects that could cause problems for their customers.

THE ENVIRONMENT

With all the concern about the ozone, global warming, pollution, acid rain, deforestation and, well, practically all aspects of our environment, people want to be environmentally appropriate. There are a number of things you can do to enhance your image in this arena—things that will position your company as an Employer of Choice in the minds of people who are sensitive to the health of the world. From roadside cleanup to environmental disaster response, companies pitch in to protect our environment.

One of the easiest and most immediate changes you can make is recycling. Even in our firm, where we simply recycle paper, glass, and aluminum, we have had employees tell us that our recycling program is one of the reasons they liked working for The Herman Group. Knowledge of recycling is so common that we don't need to devote a lot of space to telling you how to do it. We encourage you to make recycling universal throughout your organization—at all your locations. Consistency is important, or people sense hypocrisy.

> Wal-Mart sells firearms for hunting. From a social consciousness perspective, the company also vigorously supports safe hunter training programs and actively encourages gun safety.

> Tom's of Maine employees have participated in oil spill cleanups. The employees at this manufacturer of natural personal care products developed a radio program called E-Town to make people more aware of environmental issues through interviews, music, and special reports. Armed with information and understanding, listeners can make more informed decisions when buying products and may become more active environmentally.

Examine each aspect of your company's operations. Are you taking measures to assure that you don't pollute the atmosphere? Do you encourage carpooling or use of mass transit to reduce the number of cars on the road during rush hour? Do you support people working at home at least one day a week to decrease the pollution that occurs during the commute? Are there safe, secure places for employees to park bicycles if they ride to work? Are shower and changing facilities available? Has solar power been considered? What do you do to conserve energy? Are lights and equipment turned off when not in use? Do you have an ongoing campaign that emphasizes your company-wide investment in our environment?

PEOPLE

Reaching out into the local, national, and international community with aid for the less fortunate can be a plus in the social consciousness arena. Support of soup kitchens, literacy programs, clothing drives, and organizations such as Goodwill Industries fit in this category. Goodwill Industries, for example, accepts donations of items for resale, but it also runs sheltered workshops for people with various kinds of disabilities and inabilities.

Some assembly jobs, mailings, and other relatively simple tasks can be outsourced to Goodwill, helping a number of people. Clothing collection, food drives, and similar projects can make a big difference. Encouraging employees to bring in a can of food each Friday, then donating the bounty to social service organizations gives people a collective sense of doing good. The good feelings are related to their employment with a company they choose to serve. The company's outreach is congruent with their personal desires to make a difference.

> Air Mauritius, the national airline of the small island nation in the Indian Ocean, passes the hat on flights from Europe's gateway cities to Port Louis, the country's capital. Passengers are invited, on a purely voluntary basis, to contribute coins (and even bills) in the currencies of the countries from which they embarked. The funds collected are used for UNICEF programs in Mauritius. Tourist passengers are happy to donate the remaining currency from countries they've visited. A number of other airlines are following the same practice on their international flights.

INTERNATIONAL IMAGE BUILDING

International outreach can be accomplished through established programs like Operation Smile, Habitat for Humanity, and the United Nations International Children's Emergency Fund (UNICEF). The beauty of this kind of outreach is that you can involve your employees, company resources, and local community efforts, as well. These efforts don't have to be limited only to your employees.

LOCATION

The company's location is important to current and prospective employees. Many people choose their employer based on location. Some people want to live in particular locales, such as major cities, coastal areas, mountain regions, or quiet places. Others desire to work in places in proximity to things they like to do and places they like to go.

Each of us has our own preferences, so it may not make sense to move a company to another region just to attract workers. That said, we also acknowledge that a number of companies have moved out of major cities, metropolitan areas, or congested regions to seek a different quality of life. MasterCard moved from Manhattan, overlooking Central Park, to a campus-like setting in Purchase, New York, a Westchester County community. Sears moved from the famous tower in downtown Chicago to a much different environment in the suburb of Hoffman Estates. Apparel manufacturer VF moved from New York to Greensboro, North Carolina.

On a local basis, workers look for companies that are located within a reasonable commuting distance. Easy access to main highways can be a plus here, but accessibility to public transportation can be important, too. Facilities should be easy to find and well-signed. Adequate parking nearby is appreciated, particularly if it is free or at least subsidized by the employer. Would-be Employers of Choice lose points if commuters have to pay to park in order to work for the company. There would have to be some offsetting advantages to motivate a prospective employee to take a job where there's a cost for parking, instead of a comparable job in a location where parking is free.

People want to work in a safe place, in a safe neighborhood, an area where they can be comfortable. The environment should be clean, which may require employers to invest some resources in local cleanup, fix-up, and even "paint-up" work. If there are concerns about security, the employer would be well-advised to provide some sort of protective services to insure employee safety.

Many hotels and restaurants are characterized by a beautiful façade in customer or guest areas, but have a shabby, messy unpleasant area in the "back of the house" where only employees go. This differential practice is changing, though slowly, sending a message to workers that they are appreciated just as customers are. The Marriott Airport Hotel in Greensboro, North Carolina, boasts clean, bright, well-organized back areas. The far-flung operational areas of Opryland Hotel in Nashville, Tennessee, are connected by a series of well-lit, brightly painted tunnels, complete with closed-circuit televisions broadcasting company news of the day.

FACILITIES

In considering the workspace facilities themselves, employees prefer—and expect—a clean, safe, and healthy environment. For most companies, offering this type of environment is not really an issue today, though there are a number of workplaces that are not pleasant places to be. Employers of Choice will invest extra effort to be sure work areas are clean and that hazards to safety and health are eliminated. In factory, warehouse, service garages, and other work areas that are typically not envisioned as attractive and inviting, wise employers are cleaning and painting to improve the way these places look and feel.

From a visual perspective, colorful surroundings are appreciated. Studies have shown that certain colors and lighting levels are psychologically more pleasing and actually inspire higher productivity. Bright, fresh paint can change the whole "feel" of a work environment, giving workers a new sense of comfort and worthiness. They get a clear message that management cares about them. When surroundings are more cheerful, so are the people who work in them.

ENVIRONMENT

To improve physical appearance, some employers are purchasing art to create a different level of visual cheerfulness. Paintings, sculptures, hangings, and similar artistic expressions lend a sort of class to a business environment. If you don't want to invest in expensive works, visit community art shows to purchase works produced by local artists whose prices are not so high. It's a nice way to support the community, and you will probably get some positive media exposure in the bargain. Art is also available at many libraries, if you'd like to change the items displayed on a regular basis.

Check with your local high schools and colleges. Students in their art classes produce some beautiful work that would look great in your facilities. You may want to purchase some pieces, but many of these students would be thrilled just to have their work displayed in your building. They'll get recognition, the pride of having their creations shown and appreciated, and perhaps even a little money, if the art is purchased by the company, by employees, or even by visitors to the company who happen to like what they see.

Don't forget your employees and their families; you probably have more good artists in your own company family than you imagine. How about an art contest among employees? This concept might be a really special move, if it occurred in conjunction with art classes offered in the company or at a local school as an employee benefit.

> McDonald's has an impressive display of art at the company's world headquarters in Oak Brook, Illinois. Sculpture and other works are found throughout the company's campus. When Roger did some consulting for McDonald's a number of years ago, he was fascinated by the collection of art in the company's on-campus lodging facility. Replicas of a wide range of famous paintings are displayed, each with the subtle addition of a product or symbol of McDonald's.

Office arrangements and furnishings also send messages about the company and how it feels about its employees. Working in a cubicle forest is devaluing for many of today's workers. The unimaginative and somewhat sterile surroundings make them feel like commodities without the kind of individuality they prefer. Workers like to personalize their work areas. While many companies will have to stay with their cubicle arrangements for various reasons, others are moving to more innovative approaches.

Companies such as Steelcase are creating new environments like the Personal Harbor.[2] Plants—real, silk, and plastic—are being used to separate work areas, creating an "officescape" that is softer to the eye than the flat, hard surfaces of cubicles. Comfortable, less formal communication is encouraged by the placement of conversation areas with armchairs, couches, and throw pillows.

Many companies are declaring their facilities to be smoke-free. Use of tobacco is permitted in designated smoking areas only, often located outside the building. Frequently, these employers offer smoking cessation courses through their company wellness programs.

Employers of Choice are, of course, drug- and alcohol-free. Applicants with a drug problem are usually not welcome, though some employers will extend a helping hand to help people recover from addictions and start a new life.

Noise management supports the kind of working environment employees prefer. Consider Muzak[3] or a similar service, or permit each employee to listen to music with earphones, if doing so will be safe and conducive to work.

Make absolutely certain that your facilities are accessible for wheelchairs and similar needs. If you have more than 15 employees, it's the law! Evaluate ease of movement for older workers because you'll probably have more of them in the coming labor crunch. Employers of Choice will make provisions to accommodate all kinds of workers; whether they're employed at the company or not, they're welcome. It's the right thing to do.

The people of a company, guided and influenced by senior leadership, adhere to a set of values, beliefs, and behaviors that breathe life into an inanimate creature. This culture is the energy that makes a company more like a living organism. We'll explore the cultural aspects of Employers of Choice in the next chapter.

Notes

1. Wong, Nancy, "Volunteer Program is a Springboard for Career Advancement," *Workforce* Magazine, July 1999.
2. http://www.steelcase.com/products/subcategory.html?subcategory=person-alharbor&category=systems.
3. www.muzak.com

CULTURE

Just as a person can be distinguished by DNA, employers can be differentiated and uniquely identified by their organizational culture. Belief systems, the way things are done, the way people treat each other, the values and what is emphasized as being important are all part of the culture.

A McKinsey & Co. study of 77 large firms in the United States determined that 19 factors strongly influence leaders in wanting to work for an organization. Two hundred executives participated, confirming a number of the concepts we've advocated. "Values and culture" topped the list, with 58 percent of respondents saying that category was important. The next highest vote-getter was "freedom and autonomy" at 56 percent, followed by "exciting challenges" at 51 percent, and "a well-managed company" at 50 percent. Subsequent to that factor was "career advancement and growth" at 39 percent. What were the lowest vote-getters? "Job security" came in with 8 percent and "acceptable pace and stress" at 1 percent.[1]

CREATING AND MAINTAINING A UNIQUE CULTURE

Employers of Choice each have unique cultures. There is no way to say that one organization's culture is good and another is not so good. They're just different. Those differences are part of what makes employers more or less attractive—to different people. Workers have choices, so they choose the employers and cultures that are most comfortable for them: those that are most congruent with what they seek in work environments.

If employers accept that there is no one right way, no single panacea, they will design, develop, and maintain cultures that "fit" for them. The mix of a variety of rules, protocols, expectations, policies, and practices will distinguish one organization from another. In this chapter, we will present a selection of cultural attributes that are attractive to various types of employees. Employers can pick and choose which of these characteristics are important for them and for their people.

High Values and Standards

Values and standards are an important part of your corporate culture, and they are clearly visible both to present and prospective employees. The following are some ways to create a more positive and successful workplace environment.

Establish and Enforce High Standards

Establish and enforce high standards in dealings with and among employees, customers, suppliers, investors, regulatory agencies, and the world at large. An emphasis on fairness in all dealings gives people a sense of doing the right thing. In this environment, people consciously do right things. They consider whether something is right before they do it. As a consequence, employees feel that their colleagues and the company will do the right thing for them, too. This feeling can reduce stress for people who have worked for companies where they weren't sure if the right things were being done. Uncertainty about this issue, particularly among principled workers, can be very uncomfortable and unsettling.

Emphasize Ethics

When people talk about doing the right thing, ethics are a principal value. Ethics are talked about openly, with a sense of pride and concern. Moral principles guide decisions and behavior, and are sometimes even overtly based on religious beliefs. A clear sense of right and wrong is evident; the employer can insist that improprieties don't just happen. Those who deviate from the norm are quickly disciplined by management or by peers. Violations of established high standards simply aren't tolerated.

Expect People to Be Honest and Open

An expectation of honesty leads to a culture of openness and straight-dealing. While many workers find this kind of behavior refreshing and most welcome, others are sometimes quite uncomfortable with it. In such an open environment, corporate politics and game-playing don't fit. When people have something to say, they say it. There may be an increased risk of hurt feelings if people are thin-skinned, but workers quickly adjust to a culture of people saying what they mean. The risk of emotional hurt is overcome by the strong trust that people develop for each other, and for the employer.

Gays and lesbians are now "coming out of the closet" and standing up for their beliefs. Others who have been quiet about their circumstances or beliefs are likewise becoming more open. Alcoholics and recovering addicts are now more open about their conditions and the challenges they face. In Employer of Choice organizations, these people are accepted and understood. When a sales professional who is a recovering drug addict can tell her vice president that she's having a difficult day and receive understanding in return, she feels warm and secure in the corporate culture.

> A study conducted by The Hudson Institute and Walker Information, a research firm, was first published in December 1999. The results revealed that the higher employees rate their employers on ethical standards, the more loyalty they feel toward their employers and their jobs. Of the 2,300 people surveyed, 55 percent felt positively about standards and loyalty. Unfortunately, only 47 percent believe that their leaders are people of high integrity.

Eschew Mediocrity

A sense of high standards inspires people to do their work right the first time. Quality problems in this environment are not a significant issue or concern. Mediocrity is not welcome, in work, relationships, or attitudes. Superior quality is expected and enforced in all aspects of company operations. The enforcement doesn't just come from management's strict application of rules and regulations; employees themselves, as peers, monitor their own behavior and performance as well as that of others. Rather than some sort of system of spying and "tattle-tales," the workers accentuate the positive, expecting and encouraging high performance. The organization benefits tremendously from this sort of self-regulation—and establishes a sense of "this is just the way we do things around here."

Hire Only the Best

As might be expected, the caliber of workers in the environment we are describing is deliberately high. The company's selection process concentrates on attracting only the best. Those new employees who easily comply with the high-standard way of doing things are delighted to have found a home. They enjoy a company-wide mutual respect that is self-fulfilling and reinforcing. With such high standards, employees themselves will actively participate in recruiting others of equal strength and values to continue to strengthen the environment they so enjoy.

Honor Older Workers

Employers of Choice honor older workers for their wisdom, maturity, and experience. They don't try to push people out the door because they've reached the ripe old age of 55, or even 75. Whether these workers are managers, long-term assembly line workers, clerks, or truck drivers, they're appreciated for the contribution they've made to the company and to society. They are respected, sought out for counsel, and encouraged to assume formal or informal leadership roles.

Support Diversity Initiatives

The population of the United States is certainly becoming more diverse. The proportion of Black and Hispanic persons in the population and in the workforce continues to increase. Unfortunately, we have a dearth of minority persons ready to be moved into management. What this deficiency means is that employers need to make a conscious effort to solicit minorities and women to participate in management training programs, so that they will have a good representation of backgrounds in their management ranks.

Why? Because people of different backgrounds bring unique perspectives to the challenges facing the company. Greater diversity generates more breadth to planning, problem solving, and decision-making.

Encourage Fun In and Out of the Office

Life is not all serious business and nose-to-the-grindstone at an Employer of Choice. Fun must be a central part of the culture. People enjoy their work and enjoy their time with their co-workers.

Fun at work may sound like an oxymoron, but it really isn't. There are all sorts of ways to enjoy and bring out the positive aspects of work. In such an environment, there's a certain excitement as people look forward to their work, new experiences and a sense of accomplishment.

A number of companies make learning fun by holding trivia contests and offering crossword puzzles that challenge the employees to declare their knowledge about the products or services the companies offer.

Many organizations large and not so large sponsor sports teams to encourage their employees to work together outside of the office *and* to support the employees in staying physically fit.

Celebrate at Every Opportunity

Celebrations are part of the Employer of Choice culture. People enjoy celebrating accomplishments and sharing significant experiences together. Reasons to celebrate include birthdays,

---

Joyce was engaged by Bellcore in Piscataway, New Jersey, to speak at the graduation ceremony for 27 people graduating from their two-year Personal Development Program (PDP) for rising stars. She was struck by the age and cultural diversity of the group. Graduates were old and young, Black, Hispanic, Asian, and Caucasian. It seemed as if every conceivable combination of age and culture was represented. This diversity will serve Bellcore well in the coming years, as the population ages and becomes even more diverse.

When our editor, Drew Perry, was being interviewed for a job with Schwartz Communications in Boston, he was asked if he could "field." It seems the company's softball team was in need of a left fielder. His positive response to the question was instrumental in helping him get the job.

Of the 80 or so employees who worked for Schwartz, almost 25 percent participated on the team. Many others came along to cheer the players on. On workdays following games, the manager of the team would send a company-wide e-mail in the form of a sports article detailing the team's triumphs or, sometimes, varying degrees of disaster. The team was helpful in maintaining the camaraderie between employees.

Time Warner Communications, Columbus, Ohio, celebrates the anniversary of its tenured employees at the start of each monthly employee meeting. Many of the workers are pushing 10+ years with the company.[2]

individual and team achievements, meeting department or company goals, launching new products or services, anniversary dates of employment, and the company's anniversary.

Holidays serve as a platform for celebration. Halloween, for instance, stimulates costume contests, parties, and a focus on kids. The end of the year holidays—Christmas, Hanukkah, Kwanzaa—serve the same purpose. The more social and creative members of the organization will find ways to celebrate Martin Luther King Day, Presidents' Day, the first day of Spring, Easter, May Day, Memorial Day, Independence Day, Labor Day, Thanksgiving, solstices, and more.

This type of orientation does not mean that we're turning the workplace into one big, continuous party. It does, however, provide an opportunity for a break from the routine or the push for productivity. With all the stress associated with business today, injecting a little fun in the process can be quite beneficial. Studies have shown that people who take fun breaks at work are actually much more productive. They enjoy their work; they look forward to coming to work. They stay longer with the employer because it's a positive, fulfilling experience.

Develop Strong Internal Support Structures

Support people in every way possible to help them enjoy doing their work. Moral support is important, of course, but so is providing the necessary tools, equipment, materials, information, and access to perform at a high level.

When people feel well-supported, they can do a better job. They feel less stress, and are able to enjoy what they are doing. That enjoyment inspires workers to continually make a conscious—and unconscious—choice to stay with their current employer.

Make "Teamness" a Way of Life

The concept of people working in teams does not have to be directed from the top of the organization or enforced by quality improvement specialists. It happens—and should happen—naturally, at all levels. Workers create their own teams in a grass roots approach to getting things done. These teams are not institutionalized; they exist solely to accomplish particular objectives, and then they dissolve.

This pattern is contrary to what happens in so many organizations today—teams are officially formed and continue to meet long after their usefulness has expired. Result: workers complaining that they can't get their work done because they're always in meetings. Make sure that your teams are productive and useful.

Foster Collaboration

Another aspect of the Employer of Choice culture is an unquestioned ideal of working together for a common good. Departments and work groups don't compete against each other, they collaborate. Silo management is not acceptable, and matrix management is encouraged. People look for ways to help each other achieve the goals of the organization. Employers *must* make it easier for people to work closely with each other.

Meeting room environments that are conducive to sharing can make a difference. Stand-up meeting rooms—no chairs—facilitate people coming together, taking care of business, and quickly returning to their other work. Walls covered with white boards, corkboard, flip chart pads, and similar tools will help. Some organizations have found that meeting rooms with picture windows—to the inside as well as the outside of the work area—brighten up the space and open up communication. Locating meeting and gathering rooms convenient to where people work is important, too. Getting together easily should be a part of the normal way people do things, not something that is inhibited by having to

The McDonald's corporate headquarters in Oak Brook, Illinois, has no doors on the offices. The same design is found at the San Francisco public relations firm Wilson McHenry Company.

Littler Mendelson, a national labor and employment law firm with 29 offices across the United States, uses TBT to train its employees on issues such as workplace harassment and workplace violence. Developed through an allied business, Employment Law Training (ELT) Inc., the training programs teach employees core workplace values while alerting them to legal standards and obligations. The programs use a unique story-based format and a fictional workplace complete with a host of diverse characters. The user is guided through an entertaining series of vignettes that pose challenging questions and provide pragmatic solutions and guidelines.

travel to another part of the company's facilities just to meet with nearby colleagues.

A relatively new idea that produces positive results in fostering collaboration is to build conversation areas in the middle of workspaces. Couches, chairs, large pillows, and even softer lighting create a more relaxed environment for people to communicate. Arrange the furniture in a cluster, similar to the arrangement of large logs around the border of a campfire.

All for One, One for All

To stimulate the all-for-one environment, provide sufficient knowledge and insight to enable people to see both the big picture and a lot of the little pictures of what's happening. What is this "all" thing we're striving to achieve? If people don't see it, they won't "get" it. If they don't get it, they won't pursue it. And if they don't pursue it, there's no real incentive for people to work together toward those common goals or to defeat the common enemy.

Teach Core Workplace Values

Core workplace values include dignity and respect for workers, intolerance of discrimination and concern for people's safety and well being. Teaching these values not only builds a better workplace, but also is consistent with legal compliance in areas such as unlawful harassment. Employers of choice can promote these values through effective training of their workforce.

Many organizations rely on live training to educate their workers, which offers the benefits of personal interaction and group learning. Live training can be greatly enhanced and in some circumstances replaced by technology-based training (TBT). The most innovative TBT programs now offer web-based delivery, allowing employers to train their workforce through the Internet or company intranet. The flexibility of TBT makes organizing training easier, reduces costs, and allows employees, including telecommuters, to learn at their own pace in a personalized environment.

Removing Status Barriers

Most organizations have some sort of status barriers. Some are very real and deliberate. Others are more informal and not at all overt, but they still exist, and they create the same inhibitions as if they were deliberate. Employers of Choice typically send very clear messages from senior management: *We're all working together as partners to get the job done for our stakeholders. No one is any better or worse than anyone else; we simply have different roles to play in making things work.*

This kind of thinking is a natural extension of the tendency to flatten organizational structures. The flatter design was intended, in part, to bring managers closer to their people. It's worked well in many organizations; people at all levels work as one to achieve results. In other places, bosses unfortunately still tend to be bosses, maintaining a proper social distance from the people who work for them. In today's world, this posturing and separation is passé.

Relax the Dress Code

Formality in dress in the workplace is practically an anachronism in many organizations now. There has been a significant shift to a less formal dress code, which has led, in turn, to less formality in how people deal with one another. Stronger, more open communication is experienced in less formal organizations, enabling much faster, more open exchanges of ideas, problems, and solutions.

The movement to a "corporate casual" environment began with "Casual Fridays." Employees were allowed to come to work in less formal attire on Fridays in many organizations. It started as a sort of concession, even requiring monetary contributions in some companies, like an admission charge, with the money collected going to a charity or a fund for an employee party. Corporations studying the impact of relaxing the dress code for one day a week discovered higher productivity, morale, and employee satisfaction. Before long, more companies were implementing less stringent dress codes and reveling in the positive results. Shortly thereafter, informal corporate dress became more universal, all the time—not just on certain days or for special occasions.

More than 40 million office workers (53 percent) now have the option to dress casually, according to a survey of white collar workers by Levi Strauss & Company. By comparison, when a similar study was done in 1995, only 33 percent of respondents could wear business casual clothing every day, although almost one in nine could dress casually at least occasionally. In 1992, the figure was only 7 percent.[3]

When the relaxed dress code standard applies to everyone, it works best. Bosses don't wear suits, unless they have to meet with clients or have other meetings where formal attire is expected. While some organizations are very informal—tee shirts and shorts may be the norm—most establish written understandings of what is appropriate.

Eliminate the Parking Hierarchy

A status symbol—a differentiator—in many organizations has been the privileged parking space in the company lot or nearby parking garage. Enlightened employers have abolished this perk, expecting executives of all ranks to park their cars just like everyone else does. Spaces are still reserved for the handicapped, visitors, perhaps a mail car, and sometimes for the employee of the month. Some sensitive employers are now reserving convenient spots near entry doors for employees in their last eight weeks of pregnancy.

Evaluate Space Status

Traditionally, higher level bosses have been housed in corner offices, offices with windows or significantly larger cubicles. There's a movement away from this practice, giving those choice offices to teams of employees who can benefit from the shared working space and special environment. Bosses move out on the floor, closer to their people. Some bosses today share space with colleagues—to have a place to store things, hold meetings, and have a quiet place to work. Most of their time is spent away from the confines of an office—out with their people, where they can serve as more pro-active, participatory leaders.

Question the Executive Dining Room

Exclusive executive dining rooms do provide a comfortable, secure venue for private discussions. They have advantages for people working at that level. Unfortunately, when they're used as a matter of routine, they separate the leaders from the followers. Executive dining spaces, which can be a conference room, a private office area, or even an off-site location, should be used sparingly.

> All the employees at Data-Tel, a software developer in Fairfax, Virginia, have occupant identification signs outside every office and cubicle. Included on the sign is the person's name as well as icons indicating which community service projects they'd participated in and signs showing what they're doing to serve the company, like committee roles.

Executives should make it a point to eat with their people—in the company cafeteria, nearby restaurants, or wherever employees usually eat. Lunches can be pre-arranged with employees randomly—or deliberately—selected to dine with the boss. Or, bosses can just join other tables with employees, strike up a conversation, and eat together. Some organizations are sponsoring breakfasts, so bosses can eat and talk with other employees in a more relaxed, congenial atmosphere.

Reduce Formality

To facilitate open communication, change the language—the way people talk with each other. Use of first names is encouraged, supporting a sort of collegial environment. The practice of putting nameplates only on executives' doors is replaced with the practice of putting names on *everyone's* door or cubicle. Lest you think this practice is a no-brainer and out of place, we've seen a lot of companies where the bosses doors are marked, but no names are posted on cubicles to inform visitors about who occupies an area.

Provide Access to Information

People like to have information about their company, products and services, co-workers, and the industry. Having this information available helps workers feel more a part of the organizational community. If you have a company intranet, post facts and figures about things that might interest your employees. Newsletters can help convey timely information, but what we're talking about here is *institutional* information—the kind of information people need to get their jobs done.

In addition to making available a wide range of company information, let people know what's happening in your industry, in business activities in your community, with your customers, and with your suppliers. Enable them to see more of the comprehensive picture, so they better understand the environment in which you function. Inform them about trends that may affect your organization—and them.

A number of employers now engage professional speakers to deliver informative speeches, seminars, or workshops on business themes. Consider the value—educational and motivational—to your employees when they gain outside perspectives on what they're doing. On-line distance learning is picking up in popularity. Explore how these emerging technologies might enrich, stimulate, and grow your people.

Forty professional speakers formed an organization called Mentor University to provide distance learning opportunities in a variety of fields. Mentor University uses web conferencing, streaming audio, slide shows, e-mail, and other computer-based media to offer a comprehensive knowledge transfer solution to the need for more information, skills, and insights. The internet-based hub, available 24 hours, will change the economies of scale and revolutionize the delivery of corporate training, coaching, and consulting.[4]

Build a Culture of Success

Create an environment where people naturally assume that they and the company will do very well. High achievement is a way of life for Employers of Choice. Posters from suppliers like Successories can inspire the mood, but the real power comes from things the organization's leadership does and says. Setting an example, continuing to send inspirational messages and fanning the flames of a corporate spirit can make a dramatic difference. Leaders in companies that are Employers of Choice are often cheerleaders, keeping people fired up about their work, each other, and the entire team.

Fuel Excitement

We're talking about enthusiasm. This vital feeling can be grown in many ways; each organization, each leader, will determine what methods are best on an individual basis. We can't say that there is just one way of calling people to action and getting them to follow you. It's more than just the rah-rah—it's a commitment people feel from their leaders.

Leaders and their subordinate managers should be models of enthusiasm in their organizations. The way you talk, walk, engage others, attack problems, and promote good solutions all influence your people. Believe it or not, they're watching you all the time—at work, in the grocery store, at public events, even at the high school band concert. High-level leadership is a fish bowl: you're always on display. Managers are now experiencing the same things as they become more visible in flatter organizations.

Back in our high school and college days, we learned first-hand what team spirit is all about. The same methods that were used to build school team spirit then can be used to arouse corporate team spirit now. No, don't build a bonfire in the middle of the corporate offices, though you could use that approach perhaps at a local park with your employees gathered around.

Set goals and invigorate spirited campaigns to achieve those targeted results. Track progress, celebrate milestones, get people involved in the process of measurement and celebration, not just work, work, work.

Enable Public Recognition

Most people like to see their names in print—or in lights. Recognize achievements with meaningful applause and salutes that relate to the work done or the results achieved. Rejoice! Some companies have rituals that recognize people and work groups—traveling trophies, cakes, pizza, lavish dinners, incentive trips or prizes ranging from a ballpoint pen or water bottle to an exotic vacation. Recognize those who are doing a great job to make your organization more successful.

In your recognition program, make sure not to overlook the unsung heroes. Administrative support people, for example, often miss the praise that's lavished on their bosses or people they support, like sales professionals. Explore opportunities to recognize those people you depend on, whose greatest achievement may be showing up, being dependable and being productive. Every successful organization has a worthy population of people who make sure things get done, more task-oriented than recognition-hungry. Be sure to include them.

Expect High Performance

When we were teaching at the university level, we "broke the rules" about grades. Students had this idea that every class would "use the curve"—the instructor would use a bell curve to derive the scores that would be distributed in a sort of competitive fashion. A few students would get As, a few more would earn Bs, most would earn Cs—the average—and so forth. We announced to our students during the first class session that everyone was entitled to an A grade, if the recognition was earned by high performance on papers, tests, class participation, and projects. We put the power, the control of grades, in the hands of those most affected. The standards were clear. Individual achievement was up to each student.

Grades were higher than were usually earned in classes such as we taught. When people had greater opportunity for high achievement, they assumed control of their own destiny and earned the higher marks. The same philosophy we applied in the classroom many years ago applies in the workplace today. Set high standards, create the expectation of high performance, then get ready to celebrate!

Note the importance of setting standards. People will rise to their full potential, when they realize what is expected of them.

Don't allow the standards to be too conservative because complacency could result. Involve the people affected in the process of setting the standards and the objectives. People are most likely to support what they help to create.

Welcome Innovation

New ideas are fun, challenging, and stimulating. New ideas move organizations forward. New ideas keep them on the leading edge. Organizations that solicit, encourage and appreciate new ideas find themselves at the forefront of industry leadership. Business flows to them more naturally, demonstrably strengthening the bottom line.

Ensure the Availability of Resources

A lot of people have negative attitudes and have to be persuaded to think more positively and more optimistically about what can be done. Skeptics will suggest that resources like time and money aren't available, so the work can't be done. Supporting an environment of success suggests that resources *will* be available. If those resources are scarce, tell people what they have to work with—and the results they have to achieve using those resources. Often short resources can be a challenge, inspiring people to get creative to get results.

Explore attitudes and the reality of what people think—and what it really takes—to get things accomplished. Eliminate potential excuses by assuring that resources are available, that expectations are clear and that great results still have to be accomplished. It's not necessary to lavish people with every resource they need all the time. Sometimes, wrestling with a reasonable amount of adversity makes people a lot stronger.

Value Research and Development

Organizations that don't change, innovate and grow are doomed to stagnate. A stagnant organization is not a pretty sight. It's not the kind of place most people would choose to work. To become an Employer of Choice, your organization must be vibrant, forward-looking and on the cutting edge of your industry. New ideas, new products, new approaches and new ways of doing businesses fuel positive change.

If your organization is large enough to have a research and development department, shine a spotlight on the work of the special people who comprise that function. You don't have to reveal what they're working on, unless that's appropriate for some reason (such as announcing a breakthrough), but honor their value to your future. Be sure credit for your achievements, certainly those sparked by innovation, is shared with your research and development people at every opportunity. Those folks responsible will appreciate the recognition, but you will also be positioning your company differently than companies that have not made such a deep investment in this kind of work.

If you do not have a research and development arm, recognize those who are still responsible for furnishing these services for you. Depending on how you do things, there may be a couple of bright folks, usually working on other job duties, who come up with those great ideas. You may contract with an outside firm or support university research—even research of a proprietary nature. Your company's founder may be the innovator and stimulator. Whatever your particular situation, acknowledge the work you're doing that separates you from the followers in your industry. The energy and resources you invest in your future, your company's future and your customers' future differentiate you and make you an Employer of Choice.

Always be open to new ways to do things. Not all innovation will come from refinement, development, or discovery of products and services. Changing your order-taking process, your distribution system, or your marketing program, as examples, can also support your leadership position in your field or your community. Many of the people you will want to attract to work with you will choose to go to companies that are recognized leaders in their industries or communities.

Design a Successful Communication System

We're a bit hesitant to bring up this issue of communications. Practically every company that we've served as consultants over the past two decades has had "communications" problems. We've heard this word so much, we now refer to it as "the C-word." And that descriptor and attitude is more attitudinal than functional. Communications problems are an easy symptom to throw out to colleagues and consultants. The term is all-encompassing, defies description or clarification and is practically impossible to resolve using traditional approaches.

Why is this lack of definition a problem? Very simple. If you can't identify and describe a problem and its impact, it's quite difficult to solve it. So, what do we mean when we say there are "communication problems?" We see communication as a two-way street: sharing information assertively and being highly responsive to questions that may arise.

Communication involves sending messages, receiving them, understanding them and perhaps even acting upon them. Messages have to be packaged in ways that they'll be easily received and understood by the intended recipients. The messages, whether routine, special, or specifically focused, must be transmitted in ways that are appropriate for the message—content, environment, urgency, and so forth. For example, if the building were on fire, posting a notice on the bulletin board would not be effective. Nor would running through the halls shouting that the holiday schedule had been determined for the following year. The medium should fit the message.

From the recipient's side, the message must be something of interest and value *in the perception of the recipient*. The person receiving the message must believe it's important and know how to relate the information being shared to other knowledge already possessed. If there's no relationship, extra effort must be applied to the message so the recipient(s) can understand how it fits into the existing context of their lives. They must understand it and know what to do with the message they've received. See the discussion of internal marketing elsewhere in this chapter.)

There are a number of specific techniques that can be used to share information of value to employees—in ways that they comprehend the importance and utility of what's being communicated to them. Build in feedback mechanisms, and you've designed a communications system that has a higher potential for success. Let's explore some ideas.

Practice "Open Book" Management

To combat the problem of insufficient management, a number of organizations practice something called "open book management" for all employees. Jack Stack, chief executive officer of Springfield Remanufacturing Company, Springfield, Ohio, is generally credited with the origin of this practice. Essentially, the employer opens its books to all employees.

While the amount of detail shared with everyone varies from company to company, the philosophy is that all employees have access to—and understanding of—key information about how their employer is doing financially. Often, other measures such as pieces produced per hour, numbers of customers, results from marketing campaigns or changes in organizational structure or objectives are also shared. The objective is to allow all employees to see and understand what's happening in all areas of the company, as well as the company itself.

Employees are taught how to read and interpret financial statements, so they can understand and appreciate what they see on the company's balance sheet and profit and loss statement. Some companies break the budget and reporting numbers down to the departmental level, enabling department heads and their people to scrutinize what they're doing, how they're measured and what opportunities they might have for improvement.

Some organizations share this information periodically, at standard reporting intervals. Others make the information available anytime for the asking. The latter design can put a heavier workload on the accounting department, particularly if there are a lot of requests for information between regular reporting times. On the other hand, the more open policy does make a statement about the importance of understanding and collaborating.

Demand Strong Communication between Departments

Information must be shared among departments. Establish or improve mechanisms to facilitate that information sharing. In today's highly integrated departments, the work of one department can often affect a number of other departments. The more the departments are aligned, the stronger the results will be. Negative stress and frustration are minimized and everything works smoothly most of the time.

We used a rather strong word to lead off this section: demand. It's a carefully chosen word meaning to order or to require. In an Employer of Choice organization, highly effective interdepartmental communication is essential. No compromise. No ifs, ands, or buts. Strong communication is a must.

Assuring the high levels of communication that can really make a difference will be quite difficult for some organizations. Many managers, executives, and specialists are overly protective of the information they acquire and hold. Some see such information as an asset to use as leverage to gain control or influence. When this behavior is found, our recommendation to our clients is to make very clear that you are a collaborating organization of many interconnected departments and functions, not a collection of competing—or even individual—departments out for your own good or power.

To become an Employer of Choice, you must overcome the cultural beliefs that support insufficient collaboration and information-sharing between departments. The hoarding of information could be construed as such a sin that it could be grounds for termination. Show clearly the value of conscious and deliberate openness. Note that if the belief against assertive sharing is so pervasive in your organization that it will difficult to overcome, you may want to bring in a consultant or impartial outsider to facilitate some major behavioral changes.

Insist on this sharing, and let everyone in the organization know of your commitment.

Use Internal Marketing to Keep Messages Alive

Thousands of companies have spent untold millions of dollars refining the ways in which they communicate with their customers. Those same highly-polished techniques can be applied within the organization through a process we describe as internal marketing.

Consider the many methods marketers have refined over the past few decades. Included in modern marketing plans are direct marketing, regular communications such as newsletters and magazines, advertising, person-to-person contact, focus groups, interest or attitude surveys, audio and videotapes, compact discs, internet web sites, special promotions, publicity, and much more. These vehicles have been used to attract customers and keep them coming back again and again. The success of marketing efforts is evident in the traffic and sales figures that are measured so carefully in practically every organization selling goods and services to business or consumers.

These same proven methods can be used to connect with internal customers and prospective employees. The objectives of an internal marketing program are quite similar to those of an external marketing campaign; that is, they attract and build loyalty. Consider how they might be used in your environment:

- **Newsletters and magazines** can be sent on a regular basis to all your employees. The editorial content might include information about the company's products, merchandising strategies, growth of market share, stock success in the market, facilities—new, changes, remodeling—reports, sales campaigns and perhaps even research and development. People are always interested in their co-workers—marriages, children, significant events, promotions and new assignments should all be included. For more about an innovative virtual community center that started as an electronic newsletter, see the information about SoftChoice in chapter 5.

- **Advertising** internally can be done with posters, flyers, or banners promoting events, campaigns, or company philosophies. Posters and banners can be placed on bulletin boards or walls, hung from ceilings or hung on outside walls of buildings. Flyers can be distributed to work stations, put on windshields on cars in the employee parking lot, or included with paychecks.

- **Person-to-person contact** certainly works internally. People talking with people continue to feed the culture of an Employer of Choice. It's the well-known power of word of mouth. Managers and supervisors play a vital role in this technique, too. Their words and their actions manifest and reinforce the beliefs, values and commitments that bring a culture to life.

- **Focus groups** are used by an Employer of Choice to elicit employee attitudes, ideas, and concerns. Membership in these groups can come from one department or function or might represent many aspects of the organization. They can be established to gather different input from the same group on a regular basis, or similar information from different groups over space or time.

- **Interest or attitude surveys** are commonplace in business today. Employee attitude surveys are used extensively to gather input and opinions from workers. The key to success in use of this marketing technique is to share composite results with respondents. When people complete a questionnaire, they're curious about how everyone else responded. If management action is expected based on the results of the survey, preliminary action plans should be announced to employees as soon as possible after management has reviewed and evaluated questionnaire responses.

We've seen good results using a two-dimensional survey instrument. Respondents to each question indicate how they believe conditions are today, and also what they believe conditions *should* be. Comparing the *perceived* with the *desired* conditions using gap analysis techniques reveals a tremendous treasure of information to stimulate concrete actions.

> The trucking company Central Transport in Greensboro, North Carolina communicates with its drivers using a monthly audiotape. The tape features its people, president, and director of human resources delivering informational and safety messages, along with music and other entertainment.

• **Audiotapes, videotapes, and CD-ROMs** can be an effective way to provide information to employees. Trucking companies and other organizations with employees in remote locations can send consistent messages to their people using tapes or discs.

• **Satellite Broadcasts** are being used by larger organizations to communicate with their people around the country and around the globe. Use of this technology assures that the same consistent message is received by everyone.

• **Internet web sites and intranets** are a recent technological advance with exciting potential for the future. Internet sites that can be accessed by anyone can be used for sharing information with employees, families, customers, suppliers, investors and even prospective employees. Your web site, just like your product packaging and advertising, sends important messages to a wide range of stakeholders. From an Employer of Choice perspective, the quality, content and ease of use of your web site will be considered by applicants and current employees as representing what your company stands for. The better the quality, the stronger the image of the company. The worse the site, the less chance there is that prospective employees will choose you. The web has become a vitally important communications vehicle for human resources, along with other constituencies. How well is your organization using your web site as a recruiting tool?

Intranets give employees an opportunity to use internet technology to share information with each other. Department pages, lots of facts and figures, information about benefits, and so much more can be included on these sites. Just as we ask how well you use your company's web site to recruit prospective employees, we must also ask how well you use your intranet to re-recruit current employees. The employment intranet site should include everything that's on the internet site and more. Include something about how current employees are encouraged to recruit for the company and, if applicable in your organization, what kinds of bonuses or prizes are available to employees who help bring more quality people into the company.

- **Special promotions** are often used in marketing to bring heightened attention to a special sale, holiday shopping hours, new store openings, changes of management, and other events or news that may be of interest to customers. Employers of Choice do special promotions for United Way participation, employee picnics, and openings of new stores. Take advantage of these opportunities to fan the flames of enthusiasm throughout the organization, even among those who aren't directly involved in the events or the campaigns.

- **Publicity** is a means of promoting something through articles in newspapers, magazines, newsletters, radio, and television shows, as well as internet news sources. Publicity about those things that contribute to making your organization an Employer of Choice will enhance your reputation in your community. Reach out to publicity vehicles in your local community, your industry community, and in the communities to which your people belong (for instance, an article in a scouting magazine about how your company supports the scouting program).

Feature your people whenever you can; an Employer of Choice is populated proudly by people of choice.

Daimler-Chrysler Corporation provides 425,000 of its 457,000 workers in 40 countries on five continents with satellite broadcasts of news and information—in seven languages. The programming includes five minutes of auto industry news and five minutes of features about company employees, facilities, or new car models. The broadcast also includes ten minutes of text and graphics slides on new employees, company plants, and other announcements. Each facility has the capability to either add to or override the slides with some of its own. The broadcasts, which began September 1, 1999, are repeated three times an hour and shown 24 hours a day during the week. On the weekends, slides only are shown; there are no news and feature broadcasts.

A ceramics manufacturer was suffering from a serious problem with scrap and re-work. Attention was focused on how terrible this condition was and that something had to be done about it. All supervisors were required to attend a weekly meeting where the General Foreman would point out all the places where scrap was being produced, citing statistics about what it was costing the company. Over a period of time, this plant actually institutionalized scrap; they made it part of the culture! When we were called in as consultants, all we heard were negative messages about scrap; we heard no positive messages about the good work that was done.

Changing the messages people heard from management turned the situation around. Supervisors were trained in how to send positive messages, how to appreciate workers for the good work that was being produced, and how to connect on a human-to-human basis with their co-workers. The weekly scrap meeting was changed to focus on the percentage of good parts that were produced. The entire situation turned around within a few weeks. Amazing things happen when you reinforce the behavior and results you want.

Always Send Positive Messages

Continually send positive messages about sales, stock prices, quality, new customers, new employees, benefit changes, local news, personal achievements, and whatever else might be of interest to your employees. Even Susie's kid winning a writing contest in the eighth grade can be positive information to share. There is plenty of negative stuff around us every day. If we focus attention on positive things, no matter how insignificant, people will naturally think more positively and will tend to overlook the negative. No, this approach is not a Pollyanna cover-up scheme; it's a deliberate effort to accentuate the good things in our lives.

Employers who concentrate on employee retention and longevity achieve greater results than those who focus their attention on the rate of employee turnover. It's a matter of perspective. As elementary as it sounds, looking at the glass being half full is always more productive than describing it as being half empty.

Give Employees an Opportunity to Sound Off

Don't wait for the exit interview to ask people how they feel about the company, their supervisor, their co-workers, and the work they do. Solicit their ideas on how things can be done better *all the time*. Have them tell you what would make working for the company an even better experience.

Emphasize and Support Company Spirit

Provide employees with ways they can display their company spirit. Articles of clothing—jackets, polo shirts, tee shirts, sweat suits, and ball caps—with the company logo enable people to demonstrate their connection to their employer. License plate frames, coffee mugs, key rings, ball point pens, and watches also contribute to the manifestation of company spirit and loyalty.

Take advantage of charity walks, such as the Walk for the March of Dimes that takes place in many communities, to equip your people with logo merchandise. Companies that participate aggressively in such events will distribute emblazoned tee shirts and water bottles to all employees who participate. It's an inexpensive incentive that's appreciated by everyone involved. And here's a bonus: everyone else at the event sees all your employees proudly wearing their company tee shirts. It's great advertising to prospective employees—the involvement of your people is a great recruiting strategy.

RITUALS AND TRADITIONS HELP DEFINE YOUR CULTURE

Until 1997, American Freightways Corporation, a large trucking company in Harrison, Arkansas, provided employees with a suggestion box and received a whopping one or two comments a month. Management figured the response rate had more to do with the feedback method it used than employees being so satisfied that they had nothing to complain about.

To make offering comments and complaints more in line with current technology, and to bolster feedback, American Freightways began using a product called InTouch, a confidential toll-free telephone number employees could call with ideas for improvements, reports of problems with managers and colleagues, and anything else on their minds.

The results of the new system were dramatic, as 150 to 350 employees a month began calling to comment. The company still trains employees to first contact managers with suggestions and concerns, but management realizes that some employees don't feel like they can talk about some things with their bosses. This medium is another avenue for them.[5]

Employers of Choice usually have a number of rituals and traditions that define who they are, guide how achievements will be celebrated, how products will be launched, and honor people who retire. Rituals include how people are recognized, ceremonies held when people are promoted, and bonding experiences when new companies are acquired. Traditions include the family picnic held each year, executives serving breakfast on certain occasions, Christmas parties, and celebratory vacation trips to resort locations.

Modern International Graphics, Eastlake, Ohio, presented employees with sweatshirts and wristwatches sporting the company logo. Other companies, like Volvo Truck Corporation in Greensboro, North Carolina, and Dublin, Virginia, sell logo merchandise to their employees at a cost far below what they might pay for similar non-logo items in stores.

Modern International Graphics, Eastlake, Ohio, has a "nice catch" award for employees who spot a problem with a customer's printing job. When someone catches a mistake and calls it to the attention of his supervisor, the ritual begins. First, over the public address system comes the honk of a bicycle horn. Then company executives and salespeople parade through the printing plant with balloons and kazoos until they reach the workstation of the award recipient. The employee is presented with the prize—Ohio Lottery tickets. The tickets could be big winners—or not—but it's fun getting the recognition and a chance at some big money.

Manco, Inc., a manufacturer of "Duck Tape" and other products, has a culture that encourages fun as well as serious attention to business. A company ritual that endured for years captured Manco's pride, spirit, and personality: Duck Challenge Day. Each year, the company sets aside one special day to celebrate teamwork, creativity, and successes with special friends and colleagues.

CEO Jack Kahl initiated Duck Challenge Day in 1990 with a simple bet. "If we reach $60 million in sales, I'll jump in the duck pond out front." They met their goal, and Jack plunged into the icy water as the Manco partners cheered him on. From then on, a new challenge was issued each year. By 1995, 59 partners had joined Jack for a celebratory swim in the bitter cold of winter in Cleveland, Ohio.

Manco moved to its new headquarters in 1996, and the new pond was too small to continue the tradition. But Jack had a new challenge. If Manco reached $175 million, he would shave his head. Once again, the company surpassed the profit goal. Jack's haircut made headlines in business publications across the country, and even captured the attention of the *National Enquirer*.

Company-wide celebrations in a number of firms involve taking a few hours or even a whole day off work. Employees have fun together—playing games, singing, and enjoying delicious food.

Notes

1. *Workforce* Magazine, December 1998, page 55
2. Vincent Alonzo, *Incentive* Magazine, April 1999, page 26
3. *American Demographics* Magazine, April 1998, page 31
4. www.mentoru.com
5. InTouch is manufactured by Management Communications Systems, Inc., Peter Lilienthal, president. An alternative system is offered by The Network, an Atlanta-based company whose toll-free lines are staffed with live operators. On duty 24 hours a day, they can interact with employees by asking specific questions to clarify various points. The Network designed its own software program prompting operators to ask the questions to achieve as detailed a report as possible from employees.

ENLIGHTENED LEADERSHIP

Leadership is a powerful component of an Employer of Choice. Leaders make a tremendous difference every day—in their decisions, their pronouncements, their interaction with fellow employees and the clear messages they send about where the company is going, and why.

The senior leaders, those at the top of the organization, have the platform to exert the most influence. They have the position, the resources and the motivation to demonstrate the kind of leadership that can make things happen—what we call enlightened leadership. Other leaders throughout the organization, both formal and informal, also have the power to lead, support or even sabotage the company's culture and its capacity to achieve and sustain Employer of Choice status. If senior leaders abdicate their responsibility and their opportunities, the void will be filled by subordinate leaders who may or may not take the company where it needs to go. You can't take that chance.

Leaders at all levels of the organization have a job to do: leading departments, functions, divisions, plants, stores and regions to high achievement, stability and future success. Senior leaders have a responsibility to communicate their vision and expectations clearly to all other leaders. Consistency of enlightened leadership is essential for Employers of Choice; otherwise subordinates, hearing different drums, go in different directions—which could be contrary and counterproductive. Mixed messages will thoroughly confuse everyone, keeping the organization from achieving its goals. Congruent, focused messages call all team members to march to the same cadence in the same direction.

The primary factor affecting a decision to leave an organization is whether or not the manager develops a trusting relationship with the employee. This information was revealed during a survey of 500 professionals by Mastery Works, Inc, Annandale, Virginia. Over 95 percent of the respondents chose the relationship over pay and benefits. Other factors gaining over 90 percent response were the integrity of the manager, work-life balance, and career opportunities.[1]

BE FUTURE-ORIENTED

Enlightened leaders are future-oriented. They are very careful not to allow themselves to get bogged down in today's details, leaving those concerns to employees charged with operations management. Their focus is at higher levels, looking as far as practically possible into the years ahead. They set the pace, both for their company and for their industry.

As a result of their perspective, future-oriented leaders are often quoted in the media as being forward-thinking. Sometimes this happens naturally, but in most cases media relations specialists are charged with gaining positive exposure for their leaders and their philosophies. This image, which must be earned, contributes to others in the organization learning to take the risks needed to be innovative and futuristic themselves.

Future-focused leaders often bring together people of a number of diverse disciplines for discussions about what's coming. They work collaboratively to explore trends and their im-

With one eye on the future, Jacques Nasser, former president of Ford Motor Company, recognized that if he was going to be successful at taking Ford to the position of prominence to which he aspired, he would have to make some radical changes. A Lebanese-born Australian with an Aussie accent, Nasser quickly earned the moniker of "Jac the Knife" for his elimination of unprofitable divisions.

But his most drastic directives dealt with research and development. No longer could the company afford to take three to four years to introduce a new product. They would need to be able to launch in 24 months or less. While this period of two years may still seem excessive, for Ford, this compression of development time is revolutionary. This move helped Nasser make Ford significantly more competitive in domestic and world markets.[2]

plications . . . implications for society, for people, for their company. Encouraging free-thinking, they inspire colleagues to think "outside of the box" and to seek new and exciting solutions—sometimes to problems that haven't yet been clearly defined.

Leading-edge thinking and strategies are essential to success in leaders' minds, so they deliberately take steps to put themselves in that position. More than early adapters, enlightened leaders are the people who stimulate movement in new directions.

> Jack Welch, the visionary leader of General Electric, is acknowledged to have his eye clearly on the future. Although he has reorganized his company almost annually, he has the unqualified support of his people, who trust him to lead them into a successful and prosperous future.[3]

Exercise Visionary Leadership

Employers of Choice are headed by leaders who know where they're going. These leaders have a clear vision of the future, of their goals and of their objectives. They're surrounded by others who understand and support them and what they're trying to accomplish. Beyond being merely future-oriented, visionary leaders see the visions for their organizations and very deliberately lead their organizations toward the positions they want to achieve in the years ahead.

The sharper the focus, the stronger the vision will be. "We're going in that direction" is better than not knowing, but the statement, "We're going in that direction to these specific locations by these dates, and this image is what it will look and feel like" is a much more concise vision. Even if the specific vision is not attained, the organization will come a lot closer to the goal because the vision has been more carefully and clearly defined.

Communicate Your Vision to All Employees

If the vision remains in the leader's mind or office, it will not be valid for the organization. The vision needs to be shared and accepted to gain validity and the power to drive the organization.

The leader's vision can be communicated clearly in a number of ways. Followers like to hear the words directly from the leader's mouth. Words on paper can be crafted by anyone; words spoken, particularly with passion, confirm that the leader personally knows, is committed and really wants the organization to achieve the desired goals.

As the vision is explained, a process of persuasion begins. For the organization to achieve the vision, everyone has to understand it, be committed to it and know what he or she must do for the mission to be accomplished. It's not enough to paint a pretty picture. Each individual member of the team must know what is expected in terms of personal performance.

PLACE HUMAN RESOURCES AT THE STRATEGIC TABLE

An Employer of Choice is enthusiastically people-oriented. The organization's human resource is recognized as the most valuable resource. This level of recognition is reflected in the way the chief human resources officer is positioned on the organizational chart and how that executive is engaged in both strategy and day-to-day business issues.

In the kind of organization that deserves to be described as an Employer of Choice, the senior human resources executive will be integrally involved with strategic planning, design and management. No strategic move will be made without considering carefully the human resource implications, and all top executives sincerely honor the value and importance of their people.

In contrast, less enlightened leaders relegate human resources to a functional staff level. They merely take care of the paperwork necessary to remain in compliance with labor laws. People are considered to be a commodity: "If we lose some today, we'll replace them tomor-

---

Special messages sent by CEO Larry Bossidy help Allied Signal's employees located at various plants stay in touch with his vision for the company. Called "Larry's Letters," these e-mail and ink-on-paper messages clearly communicate Bossidy's plans and the importance he places on each individual worker.[4]

When the young and dynamic president of Justice Telecom, David Glickman, hired Carol Schwartz as his Director of Human Resources, he knew she would be instrumental in helping him grow the company. Together Schwartz and Glickman helped make the telecommunications firm one of Inc. Magazine's fastest growing companies in 1999.

A leading-edge thinker, Schwartz realized the need to develop an employee-centered corporate culture;

row; they're all the same anyway." In reality, while some companies still operate with the old "personnel" mentality, most have moved to a higher level. In Employer of Choice organizations, human resources will be at the highest level, reporting directly to the president or chief executive officer.

BE VISIBLE TO YOUR PEOPLE

Enlightened leaders are highly visible—inside and outside their organizations. They're active in the community, representing the employer in such a way that employees read articles about them in the local newspaper. Their work in the community generates a sense of pride among employees, and the company is well thought of because of the work being done on their behalf by their leaders.

Visionary leaders are visible in their industry, further enhancing the image that the company is a leader in the field. These active leaders also involve their people, providing external opportunities to learn, grow and make a difference.

Most importantly, enlightened leaders are seen frequently by their people. Their visibility extends beyond the occasional company meeting where employees see the guys up in front with the fancy suits. The leaders get out of their offices and go out to where their people are. They're seen, they ask questions and they listen. Employees enjoy the feeling that their leaders understand their world and are empathetic.

BE ACCESSIBLE

Beyond being visible, these strong leaders are easily accessible to their people. The open door

Glickman was willing to follow Schwartz' lead by accepting all of the initiatives that Schwartz brought to the table. Here are a few of the then state-of-the-art ideas: the day off after your birthday; on-site dog daycare (which has since evolved to dogs in the office, see chapter 5); a pumpkin-painting contest on Halloween; free lunch on payday and the day before; monthly movie nights for employees' children; regular potluck lunches; and a monthly environmental bonus to people who skateboard or bicycle to work.

Patricia Gallup is the acclaimed CEO of PC Connection, the computer mail order firm in New Hampshire. Gallup does not manage from her office, but rather often chooses to be out on the floor, close to her marketing, engineering, and sales departments. Gallup is not only visible, but approachable as well. Her people know they can really talk with her about any concern or issue.[5]

policy applies, of course, but the leaders take further initiatives to be close to their people. The techniques include hot line telephones that go right into the bosses' office—to a special phone that he answers personally whenever he can. When the boss can't take the call directly, it goes into an answering system—with the boss' voice on the greeting message—and the boss personally responds to the calls. This system is not a call center arrangement, but a personal dedication.

The CEO of Ingram Micro is Jerre Stead, who offers employees a toll-free number that only he answers. If they work in the headquarters in Santa Ana, they can visit him in his office. His glass door is always open. Not bad for the world's leading wholesaler of computer products.[6]

With the rise of electronic communication, many senior executives have special personal e-mail addresses that are used frequently by employees. Sometimes the messages express concerns or complaints, but most messages ask questions or deliver welcome endorsements and support. Another technique is for the leaders to eat breakfast or lunch in the employee cafeteria, sitting at a table large enough for a number of other employees to join in. Some executives periodically select employees at random and take them out for lunch.

REACH OUT ON A PERSONAL LEVEL

In these days of proliferating databases, we're all increasingly identified with numbers, placed in categories and generally treated more like statistics than individual humans. We crave personal attention, people relating to us for who we are. Successful leaders get to know people, call them by name, know who they really are. This kind of relationship building is a skill, and a valuable one. Strengthening this skill enables a leader to be practically charismatic.

Some leaders build strong followership by their openness and vulnerability. They talk about their families, their personal challenges and their issues. By communicating at this level, these leaders reveal their human-ness. They're people, just like everyone else. They're just playing a different role on the team . . . but they're still part of the same team. This attitude reinforces the concept of people working *with* each other, not *for* each other.

RECOGNIZE SPECIAL OCCASIONS

Each of us has a birthday to celebrate—once a year, every year. We celebrate important events like our wedding anniversaries, the date we joined the company and children's birthdays. These dates are important to us. If we get a card, a phone call, a letter, flowers or even a gift from someone to celebrate the occasion with us, it's special.

Leaders, even leaders of very large organizations, can recognize these special dates in the lives of their valued employees. The investment is minimal, but the return is huge. Such involvement sends a clear message of caring, the kind of message that strengthens bonds and builds a strong sense of community within the organization.

Don't overlook celebrating special occasions like the anniversary of the company's founding. This event can be a festive time as well as a meaningful time. It can be a time of rededication and renewal that energizes people and the organization to help keep you moving forward.

Involve the family. Send cards and letters home on special occasions. Recognize the contribution that family support makes to employee success. This appreciation is especially important after workers have invested extra time in a project—traveling or working overtime—that kept them away from their families.

ENCOURAGE AND EMBRACE CHANGE

Change can be frightening for a lot of people, particularly as fast as changes are occurring today. The right kind of change can be very positive, making a positive difference for all concerned.

Following the lead of Domino's Pizza former CEO Tom Monaghan, each manager spent whatever time it took to review with each employee a form called job-planning and review (JP&R). The purpose of these meetings was to discuss the subordinate's dream or mission and help people realize their individual goals.[7]

Mary Kay Ash, the charismatic founder of Mary Kay Cosmetics in Dallas, Texas, knows that her people appreciate her attention to special occasions. They tell her so. She personally signs every birthday and anniversary card sent to her employees. She also recognizes other special occasions. New babies receive little silver banks in the shape of ducks. She acknowledges weddings with silver bowls. Employees receive free lunches (for two) or free movie tickets on their birthdays. Plus, employees receive a $100 savings bond for every five years of service.[8]

Part of the role of an enlightened leader is to advocate wise change, to encourage people to look for ways to do things better, faster and easier. Leaders also interpret outside changes for the organization, analyzing and evaluating what current and future changes might mean to each employee and function.

Embrace change. It's going to happen anyway. If you, as a leader, welcome change and facilitate it within your organization, you will help to keep people flexible, adaptable, and resilient. Employees and applicants know things are changing, and they'll consciously choose the employers that can respond well and even lead the change. Companies that are rigid and resisting change may be doomed for extinction. When they have a choice, people don't want to work for those kinds of organizations.

DELIVER OPEN AND HONEST FEEDBACK

People want to know how they're doing. If they feel they're in the dark, if they're not getting good feedback, they'll choose to go somewhere else to work. Be straight with people. Avoid playing games with them. Direct, open, honest feedback, delivered on a continual basis, is genuinely appreciated. Don't wait until scheduled appraisal interviews, but share your feedback in a timely manner.

Feedback should be communicated in a constructive manner. The objective here is not to criticize, but to help. When people are doing things well, tell them what you like, why you like that behavior or performance, and what difference it makes. When someone isn't doing quite what you want, explain what you're looking for and what you perceive the errant employee is doing. Check to be sure you're sharing the same perceptions about what's happening. Describe what behaviors you'd like to see and help the worker perform in the desired fashion.

In Employer of Choice organizations, people will freely share feedback with each other, at all levels, with a mutual sense of helping everyone perform better. That improved individual and team performance will help the entire organization. People prefer to join, and stay with, employment environments where the philosophy is "all for one and one for all."

BE RECEPTIVE TO FEEDBACK FROM OTHERS

Receptivity to feedback might be considered a given in an Employer of Choice organization. It might surprise you how many leaders don't respond well—or at all—to suggestions about how they, or the organization, might do better.

Executives should respond promptly to ideas, criticisms, and other input. Sometimes this response will be direct, particularly if the input came from one person or group and was directed at one leader. In other cases, the response will be more broad, using mass e-mail, intranet posting, bulletin board announcements, or similar vehicles to convey the message.

The secret is to respond in a timely manner so people know they've been heard. While they're looking for some kind of action in most cases, they really want to know that someone is listening to them—that their opinion and their voice matters.

> To solicit ideas for his new employee-oriented policies, Vernon Hills, Illinois, CDW Chief Executive Officer Michael Krasny gave every employee five stamped envelopes, addressed to him. The ideas he received helped him to quadruple sales over the last five years. Employees are also impressed that Krasny is not afraid to stack boxes with his people in the warehouse.[9]

CREATE AN ENVIRONMENT OF CARING COACHING

Coaching and mentoring have become increasingly popular in work environments. Today's employees want to be mentored, and they want to be coached to higher and higher performance and achievement—personally and professionally. Enlightened leaders will encourage these positive relationships as part of the sense of community of mutual caring and support.

Mentors and protégés usually connect informally, rather than becoming linked through a formal corporate program. Some companies have established formal assignment and tracking programs for mentorship, with varying results. We prefer arrangements where protégés personally select and invite people to be their mentors. The motivation seems stronger on the part of both parties. In the mentoring relationship, the protégé seeks out the mentor when help, advice, or counsel is needed. The onus is on the protégé.

In the coaching relationship, the coach assumes more responsibility for monitoring and intervention. The protégé is more involved with the process than in a typical supervisor-subordinate relationship, and the coach may well get into more issues than strictly on-the-job performance concerns. Sometimes supervisors serve as coaches; in other cases, coaching is provided by human resources, training, or organizational development professionals, or perhaps trained volunteers from other departments. Professional coaches from outside the organization may be quite appropriate, especially if the people being coached are executives or senior managers. The coaching profession emerged in the mid-1990s, with a significant number of executive coaches being graduates of Coach University (www.coachu.com).

TRANSFER, PROMOTE, TERMINATE

Employer of Choice organizations provide plenty of opportunities for people to learn, grow, and reach for their full potential. Today's workers are restless. They don't want to work at one job for more than 2–3 years. They often want to change jobs, but not necessarily employers. They want to different kinds of work, rather than be constrained to one kind of work for their entire career.

People employed by preferred companies are able to transfer relatively easily from one department to another and from one function to another. They can move geographically, as well, to take advantages of multiple opportunities within the organization. They choose to stay with the employer because they are able to do the kind of work they like to do. They can experiment with other kinds of work without having to change jobs or putting their careers at risk.

Astute employers today are conscientiously removing "dead wood" from their midst. Over the years, non-performers or marginal employees have been able to hide in the organization, keeping their jobs and their paychecks without significantly contributing to the company's success. Few employers can afford that luxury anymore, so nonproductive employees are being sought out and given career redirection opportunities.

Removing people who should no longer be on the payroll opens opportunities for current and future employees to move into the vacated positions. It also sends a clear message that the organization will no longer tolerate substandard members, lending positive reinforcement to all those valued employees who work so hard every day.

DISDAIN CORPORATE POLITICS

In so many environments, we've heard how politics influences decisions, career opportunities, and even productivity and profit. While recognizing that some political issues will always be there, Employers of Choice seek to drive all the negative attributes of organizational politics out of the culture. People are assigned and promoted on their qualifications, merit, and proven abilities, rather than on the basis of who they know, how long they've been around, or who owes who favors.

Savvy executives remain vigilant in an ongoing hunt for political games in the organization. When they find this kind of behavior or maneuvering, they stop the practice or find out why it's happening. This knowledge is used to create and maintain a more open organizational culture.

FACILITATE HIGH PERFORMANCE

The strength of your organization lies in your people—in each individual employee. Today's worker is more independent, more driven to initiate and follow through on his own, instead of waiting for direction from management. People choose to work where they have opportunities to do things on their own, to make things happen, to assume a certain amount of control, and to feel a sense of personal accomplishment in their own achievements.

Continually seek ways to enable people to work on their own and to form their own teams to complete specific tasks. Recognize individuals for their work and provide learning opportunities and other kinds of support for people eager to do things independently. Keep those energetic individuals focused on the company mission statement and monitor performance expectations to assure they stay on target.

Advocate strong support for front-line employees so they can get their jobs done. Turnover is often highest among entry level employees and recent hires. Provide training, tools, equipment, materials and encouragement for these important workers, and you'll minimize the possibility of their leaving prematurely. With greater stability in this component of your workforce, other employees will find their work is smoother, building a company-wide sense of stability and continuity. Most workers prefer this kind of environment, so you'll enjoy wider benefits from some focused effort.

PUSH ACCOUNTABILITY DOWN THE LADDER

One of the problems with most organizations is that accountability rests at too high a level. The secret to high performance is to push accountability down as far as possible, preferably to the front-line, hourly employees. People want to be accountable, so this strategy is congruent with what employees desire.

When the employees who are closest to the work assume accountability for what's happening and for what's produced, managers no longer have to worry about all those little details. They are able to concentrate more on what they need to do to support their people, coordinate among departments and generally keep things moving. When the company "machine" runs more smoothly, stress is lower. The company becomes a nicer place to work, and more people will choose to be there.

WELCOME NEW HIRES

The investment to find, attract and hire new employees can be significant. If you don't hold on to these people, you'll have to continue recruitment at a high level—a costly proposition. If you're doing an effective job in selection, you'll add just the right kinds of people to your organization. It makes sense to follow through with your investment to assure that the highest percentage of people possible continue as long-term employees.

Supervisory leadership plays a vital role here, but so do leaders from higher up in the organizational chart. The more welcome people feel, the more likely they are to remain. Group meetings, individual interviews, visits to work stations, phone calls, welcome cards and similar gestures all make a difference. Arrange for communications to occur at intervals that your experience tells you have the highest vulnerability for turnover. In other words, if people tend to leave soon after they've been with you for six months, initiate more intense, welcoming, inclusive communication starting at about the five-month point. Build commitment by reinforcing the feeling of belonging among *all* employees.

CHAMPION EMPLOYER OF CHOICE CONCEPTS

The human resources department should strive to build the Employer of Choice environment and work to establish the reputation in the marketplace. However, to be real, to be effective, the Employer of Choice concept needs strong, active support from senior executives and senior leaders.

Leaders should talk about the various aspects of the Employer of Choice concept at every opportunity—to large groups, small groups or to individual employees. Speak with pride, with inspiration and with excitement. Enthusiasm is contagious, and success will build on success. Once a program gets moving, momentum will carry it forward.

ENGAGE AND SUPPORT AN OMBUDSMAN

As people engage in their busy corporate lives, they run into situations that might be best handled by someone who can cut through all the

When speaking to a university class one day, David Russo, head of human resources for the SAS Institute, was asked why SAS does so much family-friendly stuff. His reply demonstrated how doing the things that make a company an Employer of Choice also make sense economically. Russo's reply: "We have something like 5,000 employees. Our turnover rate last year was 3 percent. What's the industry average?" Somebody said 20 percent. Russo replied, "Actually, 20 percent is low, but I don't care. We'll use 20 percent. The difference between 20 percent and 3 percent is 17 percent. Multiply 17 percent by 5,000 people, and that's 850 people. What does turnover cost per person? Calculate it in terms of salary." The students calculated the cost of turnover per employee to be the cost of one year's salary, and noted that the average salary is $60,000. Russo said, "Both of those figures are low, but that doesn't matter. I'll use them. Multiply $60,000 by 850 people, and that's more than $50 million in savings."

That's how Russo pays for the SAS gymnasium, for on-site medical care, for all of the company's other family-friendly items. "Plus," he said, "I've got tons of money left over." If you can save $50 million a year in reduced turnover, you're talking about real financial savings.[10]

red tape, someone who can move across all the organizational lines. We call this problem-solver an ombudsman. Employed by a number of companies, often as an outsider, an ombudsman serves as a change agent, a mediator and a stimulator of actions needed to resolve troublesome issues.

With direct access to the chief executive officer and everyone else in the organization, the ombudsman can break down barriers to achievement and communication, reinforce the corporate culture and build a greater sense of trust and collaboration. As an impartial consultant to all, he or she takes the initiative to move things forward when organizational protocols make it difficult for others to take a lead position.

Assure that the person chosen to be the ombudsman understands the culture, mission, values and objectives of the company. The CEO's openness and support will help this key player become highly effective in eliminating inhibiting problems or systems to bring the organization to a much higher level of performance and stability. The list of companies offering ombudsmen includes Rockwell, Johnson & Johnson, Herman Miller, Volvo, Morley Builders, and Pan Pacific Hotels.

INSPIRE SERVANT LEADERSHIP

Servant leadership is defined as a style in which the leader considers himself a servant, a support, to other employees. Under this concept, the role of the leader is to serve all employees so they can perform their jobs and fulfill their responsibilities.

While this design is advocated by many, it is difficult to implement. As they rise through the hierarchy, many leaders acquire an ego that screams to be fed. The servant leader subjugates his ego, seeking to serve rather than direct. Emphasis is placed on individual and group achievement and initiative, with leaders setting the tone, the direction and the vision. Servant leaders can then begin asking questions like, "How can I help you accomplish your objectives?"

Once these leadership directives are established and are firmly in place, you can then turn to the direct and specific care of your people, as discussed in the next chapter.

> Deanna Pardi is Vice President and Branch Manager for Dearfield Associates, Inc., in Phoenix, Arizona. Dearfield, an outbound telemarketer, is in the enviable position of turning down more business than it accepts, preferring to work for large, well-respected, blue chip companies whose philosophy is aligned with theirs. Pardi credits part of her success to her discovery of a small book, To Lead is to Serve, written by Shar McBee.
>
> Pardi believes that it's management's job to serve the employees. Management serves the employees by "looking for and bringing out the best in each individual, by supporting individual growth and development, by listening, by giving value to our employees, and by providing meaningful rewards." The average turnover for the call center industry is over 150 percent; their's is a fraction of that.[11]

Notes

1. *Talent 2000—Retention and Development for Managers*, Mastery Works, Annandale, Virginia, July 28, 1999.
2. "Ford's Heir-Apparent is a Maverick Outsider," by Robert Simison, *Continental*, April 1998 (reprint from *The Wall Street Journal*), pp. 57–58.
3. "Six Sigma," Hal Clifford, *Continental*, November, 1997.
4. "100 Best Companies," *FORTUNE* Magazine, January 11, 1999, p. 140.
5. "Leadership for the Millennium," by Esther Wachs Book, *Working Woman* Magazine, March 1998, p. 31.
6. Ibid, p. 140.
7. "Tête à Tête," *Inc.* Magazine, April 1998, p. 74.
8. *The 100 Best Companies to Work for in America*, by Robert Levering and Milton Moskowitz, pp. 269–270.
9. "100 Best Companies," *Fortune* Magazine, January 11, 1999, p. 130.
10. "Danger: Toxic Company," by Alan M. Webber, *Fast Company* Magazine, November 1998, p. 152.
11. "Dearfield Associates bucks the trend," by Deanna Pardi, *The Workforce Stability Alert*, November, 1998, pp. 2–3.

CARE OF PEOPLE

People are your most valuable resource. And those people make choices *every day*. They choose whether to go to work for an employer; they choose whether and how to work while they're there; they choose whether to stay with that employer. Wise employers will invest time, attention, and all sorts of other resources to take care of their people.

Quality of life is a major issue for people in all walks of life. They want to feel comfortable and serene. They want to feel good about themselves, their lives, and their future. With all the pressures in work environments, more and more workers are exclaiming that they want more out of life than just work all the time. They want time for other things in their lives—family, personal development, health and fitness, community activities, religious learning and observance, and time just to be quietly alone.

Each of us defines quality of life differently, so we can't, within the workplace, circumscribe a specific set of criteria. The key, then, is to create an environment where each employee can determine for himself or herself what constitutes a good quality of life—then create what they want for themselves. Perhaps the solution is flexibility and accommodation. Perhaps part of the solution is for the company to support quality of life programs.

CORPORATE SUPPORT

Corporate support of quality of life programs can include sponsoring a company bowling league, tickets to a concert series or sporting events, baby photo contests, exercise facilities, automated teller machines (ATMs), or soft drink machines with discounted prices. Some employers provide rooms where new mothers can express milk, or even breast feed their babies if company policy allows them to bring the infants to work with them.

More common issues may involve employees' being able to take some time off to join a grandchild at school for bring-a-grandparent-to-lunch day or to care for a sick child at home. Time is a vital commodity for today's workers, and will become more important as the years go on. Trend indicators clearly show that people don't want to work "24/7." There are too many other things for them to do in their lives. We've come a long way from the period when the only major activity was the hoe-down on Saturday night.

Some of your employees will still have difficulty maintaining balance in their lives. They'll be unhappy, but won't know why. And they'll tend to blame their unhappiness on their employment situation and will leave your employ in a futile search for serenity. Help them in their search—while they're still on your team.

Refine your concern *about* quality of life to concentrate *on* quality of work life. Build fun and variety into the work experience. Create an environment that invites people to come to work. In short: build a place that people want to be.

How to Improve the Corporate Environment

Some things you can do to take care of people are customary and expected in most companies. We'll include some of them here as reminders; some of those taken-for-granted measures may need some refinement and upgrading. Each of the ideas we'll share in this chapter have been shown—through research and/or actual application—to be valued by employees. As people determine the kinds of things they want in their work environment and in their relationship with their employer, many of the techniques described in this chapter will be included on their lists.

Some of these ideas may seem a bit unusual. But, remember that attracting, optimizing, and holding good people is a competitive activity. Those unusual approaches may just capture the attention you need to win the people you want and to keep the people you'd like to stay with you.

Advocate Work-Life Balance

We'll start with work-life balance, since this issue is getting a lot of attention. We've moved through an era where people devoted whatever time was necessary to work. A significant proportion of our workforce has long worked a considerable number of hours, sacrificing time with their families and friends—and themselves—to meet the needs of their employers.

During the period when there were more workers than jobs, putting in the long hours of hard work was a wise way to build job security. Those who could be counted on got the jobs, enjoyed the preferred assignments, and usually kept their jobs when layoff time came. These people are tired and feel that they deserve some time at home. Yet, these are the key people who are needed by their employers, especially during these times of a high volume of orders and insufficient people to fill them. "Enough!" these people are saying. "I want a break. I don't want to work all the time anymore."

Younger employees also want time for themselves and their families. They're reluctant to even get into the long hours thing, preferring to check out after 8 to 10 hours to take care of the personal side of their lives.

Ann Price, CEO of Motek in Beverly Hills, California, is the strongest advocate for work-life balance we know. Since Motek is located in the land of giant freeways, which serve as parking lots 6 hours per day, Price jumped on the idea of telecommuting. What happened surprised her and us. She often visited her employees in their home offices and was taken aback with what she observed. Many of her employees had pictures of other Motek employees on their desks.

Few employees, including Price, came into the office on a daily basis, so the office space was small. The office was used as a hub and the location of their monthly meetings, and Price wanted employees to have their own desks whenever they needed to be in the office. Within a year, almost all of the employees had relocated closer to the office and were coming in on a daily basis. Price had not dictated any policy; people simply decided for themselves that they wanted to work more closely with each other in the office environment.

Price was not concerned about her telecommuting employees working enough. She was concerned about them working too much. She knows that life-balance is an important element to having happy, productive employees.

Motek's corporate culture supports people walking to work. One of their employees who used to commute at least two hours on the freeway each day now lives one block from the office and walks to work. She believes the quality of her life has substantially improved. The company also helps find housing for any employee who wishes to abandon the Los Angeles freeways and walk to work.[1]

Carol Schwartz, Director of Human Resources at Justice Telecom in Culver City, California, called herself "the Work Police." Shortly after Schwartz started working with Justice, she discovered that some employees had erected "tent cities of blankets and were camping out on the floor, sleeping overnight at the offices." She decided that the young techies needed to balance their lives better. Schwartz would return to her offices at 11:30 P.M. or midnight and send them all home.

Demonstrate Respect for the Individual

Today's worker wants individual attention and personal respect. There's an underlying feeling in the corporate world that workers have not received the respect they deserve from supervisors, managers, and even co-workers.

One way to demonstrate respect is to ask people for their input and their opinions, rather than just telling them what to do. This approach recognizes that workers have a lot to offer in terms of expertise and experience. When you value what they have to say, you convey respect.

Tell your employees about changes that are coming, letting them in on things before they become official. As much as possible, be sure your employees know about company news at the same time or even before you announce it to the media. No one likes finding out about something that affects their work in the newspaper. By telling reporters before you tell your employees, you send a message that the media people are better—more important—than your own people. To avoid leaks, give your employees information at the same time the media is notified.

Encourage Workers to Recruit Their Friends

Although most employers would love to have their employees recommend their friends for jobs within the company, relatively few invite them to do so. Don't just expect it, but aggressively encourage workers to recruit. They'll be recruiting their co-workers: the people they can depend on.

Managers at a number of consumer-service companies—retailers, restaurants, restaurants, and similar establishments—have cards, similar to business cards, that they can hand to workers they see when they're shopping, eating out, traveling or just trawling for workers. The cards tell a little bit about the company and include a special phone number to call for further information or an application. In today's world, a web site URL should be displayed, as well. The employee should also put his or her name on the card.

There's no reason that such cards can't be given to all of your employees. They can give them to friends, to neighbors, to fellow parishioners at church, and to workers they see as they go to stores or visit other places. Human resource professionals answering the special phone number should give extra attention to these referrals, acknowledging that they came as a result of contact with a valued company employee.

An increasing number of companies have established bonus programs, paying cash to any employee who refers an applicant who gets hired and stays with the company for some length of time. Six months seems to be a popular threshold. Some companies reward the new employee as well, with post-sign-on bonuses at 6-, 12-, and perhaps 18-month anniversaries. Consider offering bonuses (perhaps we should call them "bounties") to customers or suppliers who help in recruiting.

Create a Home-like Environment

The physical environment people work in is im-

Ericsson, Inc., Lynchburg, Virginia, makes cellular telephones, marine radios, and related products. Ericsson has tremendous respect for its individual employees. Not only does the company encourage employees to submit suggestions for improvement, it recognizes and rewards those suggestions with goodies and accolades. In addition, each team has a television monitor that is continuously televising company news and other important information. They want to keep their employees informed and happy.

The Cheesecake Factory, a 28-store restaurant chain based in Calabasas Hills, California, has enjoyed great success since Bill Streitberger, Vice President of Recruiting, joined the company a little over a year ago. Streitberger asserts that referral programs can either be a burden or they can work beautifully. The secret to success is simple: be creative and persistent.

Streitberger is concerned with hiring management personnel and hourly workers to fuel the company's stability and growth. The company's bonus programs are different for the different types of recruits, of course. He offers a $1000 bonus for each manager hired. And he doesn't care to whom the bonus is paid. Other managers? Fine. Other employees? Also good. Next-door neighbor? Sure!

Streitberger explains that $1000 is an inexpensive investment for a good new hire. He likes to run the program without restrictions he finds inhibiting. His focus is on finding good people. The idea is to make it attractive for people to make recommendations! Under Cheesecake Factory guidelines, an applicant must initiate the phone call. Streitberger observes that this requirement helps him avoid cold calling . . . and the incoming call demonstrates an applicant's genuine sign of interest and assertiveness.

How long do these new managers stay? Streitberger reports that after a year, not one person hired under the system has left. Retention is at 100 percent!

A less lucrative version has been effective in attracting good people to work in hourly positions in Cheesecake Factory locations. The amount of bonus paid is at the discretion of the General

portant to them. The appearance of the company's facility, the colors on the walls, the kind of furniture, the noise level (and perhaps music), light, temperature and ventilation are all significant.

Office workers enjoy an environment where they can display pictures of family, favorite places, pets, or something having to do with their hobbies. When they gather with co-workers, to take a break or to meet about some business, they like a comfortable place to be. Meeting rooms with ergonomic chairs, break rooms with decent furniture, or conversation pits with sofas and throw pillows can be effective gathering spots.

To soften the physical environment and to move away from the typical stark, flat nature of workspaces, use color and plants. If you can't get plants to grow in your closed environment, use plastic or silk plants to create the effect you want. Soften the lighting and create spaces with more curves than corners. Carpet, art—two-dimensional, sculpture, or something creative—changes the way the workplace "feels."

Bring in some of the other comforts of home, such as a refrigerator for people to store food, storage areas for plates and cups, and some furniture that doesn't look like it belongs in the stereotypical business office.

Remember: work to change the stereotypical workplace.

Consider how some of these same benefits can be offered to workers who are not office-based. Many of these features can be installed in factory or warehouse environments or in back-of-the-house spaces in hotels, restaurants, or retail stores. Once you are focused on what can be done for employees, you can decide better how and where to make your investment.

Maintain a Safe, Healthy Environment

Emphasizing safety and health in the workplace is certainly appreciated by workers. The National Safety Council (NSC), located in Itasca, Illinois, is a nonprofit, non-governmental international public service organization dedicated to improving the safety, health and environmental well-being of all people, on and off the job.

The NSC urges, as do we, that you support safe working habits and a safe workplace. The use of posters and reminders are a part what can be done. Talking about safety, watching for hazards, disciplining employees for deliberately unsafe practices, and fast response to incidents will show a genuine concern for a safe workplace. Information and support materials are available from NSC's web site at www.nsc.org or by calling 630-775-2231.

Manager of the restaurant, but is paid to both the employee who made the recommendation and the new hire.

The company assumes full responsibility for the quality of the people hired. "Once we make the decision to hire, it's our job to inspire the new employees to stay." That's why the bonus is paid to the new hires quickly—as soon as the new workers have completed their initial training, typically a week or two.

Company employees carry recruiting business cards and are encouraged to recruit. "We want the program to be fun and interesting, with attainable rewards. We want to pay the money—the result is a good, cost-efficient hire."[2]

Bob Noble, President and CEO of Noble & Associates, the largest advertising agency in the country that's devoted to the food industry, calls his firm, "a company that the client built." Noble believes that the open architecture layout of his offices is a reflection of their client focus. He describes his employees as "talented individuals who have embraced brand-building and are very keen helping clients keep their businesses ahead of the changing marketplace." In order to keep clients ahead of the changing marketplace, they needed to be more nimble, get work done more quickly, and shorten the time between project inception and completion. They also needed to provide the same services for less money but deliver more value.

Using the metaphor of the solar system, the organization eliminated layers of management and divided the company into teams. Its teams all have astronomical names, like the Milky Way, Mercury, Venus, and Saturn. Serving all the other heavenly bodies is Earth which includes information technology, accounting, human resources, and other universal services to all the teams.

Basically, the company created a group of small agencies to offer an umbrella of services; now the quality client teams offer one-stop shopping. The smaller agencies cross over between functions and therefore have reduced the number of steps and improved processes to shorten completion time. There's no more traffic department; each team handles its own traffic. This arrangement works well for disseminating information throughout the organization.

To support the teams' working arrangements, Noble developed an office layout that is so flexible that it can be reconfigured within minutes to allow groups of employees to collaborate or work independently. There are no walls. All partitions and desks are on wheels; all phone jacks and outlets are in the floor. Each planet space has two to four conference rooms and one to two telephone booths to allow for complete privacy with personal calls. Of course, comfortable congregant spaces that promote collaboration and creativity are an important aspect of this design.

Noble encourages "intrapreneuring," among his employees, allowing the teams to buy the services of other team members at inside rates, when the employees are not otherwise occupied with their own clients' work. Noble's gain sharing program has an astronomical name, too—COMET (Contribution Over Minimum Established Targets) Pay. To foster teamwork, Comet Pay is only distributed when the entire solar system has reached its assigned threshold of profitability. Is it working? In fact, the new system is exceeding expectations. The clients are happy and so is the agency.[3]

Consider having your building(s) and grounds checked periodically for environmental hazards. Asbestos has received much attention, but there are other concerns as well. Be alert to the use of pesticides in the care of the green areas that surround your facilities. Most of your work in the area of safety will involve raising awareness and monitoring. If people who work in your buildings are becoming ill at work, check their environment to be sure it's a healthy place to work. Respond quickly to any problems that might indicate a problem area to be investigated and managed. It is always better to act than to react.

Many companies offer incentives to individuals for clean safety records. Some offer a drawing for all of the employees who work in a plant that has been accident-free for a period of time. Others offer bonuses and incentives to truck drivers who remain accident-free.

> Farm Fresh Bakery in Lawton, Oklahoma, has a safety program that's one of the best in their industry. One of the reasons for their enviable record is that the company rewards the employees for accident-free months and years with raffles and drawings. Employees have won pick-up trucks, washers, dryers, cash, and other items the committee deemed appropriate.[4]

Foster Good Working Conditions

The concept of good working conditions is a given, but what does that mean? People like a clean, well-organized workspace. They want to know that they can find things when they need them and that equipment will be in good repair. Arrange furniture and work flow in ways that make sense—ask the people who actually work in those areas how things should be arranged. After all, they'll know best what they need.

Ensure that work is organized so that people know what they're supposed to do and what others are supposed to do. When people understand the total flow of their work, they can become more dedicated to getting their parts done. Working conditions, for our discussion, also include the systems people use to accomplish tasks.

Avoid getting too heavy-handed from the top of the organization regarding how work should be organized—either in flow or in location and relationship to workers. People want to manage these things themselves, rather than be told what to do by someone who may not know the situation as well as they think they do. If you do have to intervene, do so with questions that stimulate thought and discussion. Give people a greater sense of control over the conditions under which they operate.

Provide the Right Equipment

Our research suggests that today's workers really want to do a good job. They want to excel in everything they do. When they can't achieve high performance, they can become frustrated and quit. One of the frustrations workers experience is not having the right equipment to get their job done. Whether it's a large piece of manufacturing machinery, a delivery truck, a cash register, a vacuum cleaner, or a computer, it's a pain in the neck when it doesn't work right—or when it's not there at all.

To support your people, ensure that the right equipment—in their perception—is available to work with, and that the equipment works properly. Purchase or lease what's needed, then service the item(s) regularly so that everything stays in fine operating condition. At the same time, be sure that everyone has the materials needed. Let nothing hinder high performance.

Encourage Relationships Among Employees

People who work for Employers of Choice choose their co-workers as well as their employer. Reinforce that wise choice by encouraging friendships among your people. Give them opportunities to be together socially, both within the work environment and outside the workplace.

Within the work environment, conversation areas, break rooms, cafeterias, and similar gathering areas are conducive to people meeting person-to-person. Outside picnic tables, exercise areas, and

Normally, visiting the emergency room of a hospital is not a very pleasant experience. But this unpleasantness is not the case at St. Barnabas Hospital's Emergency Department in Livingston, New Jersey. Managed by Dr. Jay Kaplan of Emergency Medical Associates (EMA), this facility has television sets in each cubicle for the waiting patients to watch. Naturally, these diversions reduce the stress levels for the employees, because they are not dealing with irritated patients who have been waiting for attention.

But televisions for the patients are only a small indicator of the dazzling array of technology that the organization provides to make the employees more efficient. There are machines that take the patients' temperatures, blood counts, and blood pressures—with minimal effort on the part of the healthcare providers. To the degree that it is possible, EMA uses technology to automate the busywork functions for its workers. So how does this investment in technology affect the employees? EMA has very low turnover, and in the healthcare field, that condition is unusual.

park-like space on your grounds make it easier for folks to get together and just be. No pretense, just people.

Serving a continental breakfast each day, or perhaps one day a week depending on your facilities, might be a consideration. That breakfast doesn't have to be anything fancy—just beverages and doughnuts, muffins, pastry, and perhaps some fruit will be well-received. The cuisine is not as important as the opportunity for employees to join together informally to have a munchie and a cup of coffee in a relaxing environment before work begins.

The same approach can be used for breaks— pre-planned or spontaneous. Short parties to celebrate birthdays and similar events encourage human-to-human relationships.

Outside of work, consider sponsoring picnics, dinners, retreats and even Outward Bound-type experiences like ropes courses. Scavenger hunts, trips to trade shows, vacation and incentive trips, and similar activities create situations where people can talk about more than just their focused work.

Champion Flexibility in All Forms

Today's employees want flexibility in their lives, as well as their work lives. They don't want to be tied down by schedules, silly rules, procedures that used to work, or rigid requirements of any kind. People want flexibility in the way they do their work, particularly if they have the expertise to get the job done without overbearing instructions from above.

Explore a range of flexible schedules and time-at-work policies. Get your employees in-

Arthur Andersen in St. Louis, MIssouri, employs interns. Offering internships helps predispose the young people to working full-time for the company. Through Dick Hall Productions, the corporation sponsors a "game night," their own version of the old game show, *Truth or Consequences*.

The contestant-students are asked general information questions. Incorrect answers earn cream pies in their faces. It's messy, but lots of fun for the students. And of course, they win prizes—even when they fail the to give the right answers. Throughout the evening, the students are interacting with Andersen employees and the employees are connecting with each other.[5]

When Newell Rubbermaid in Freeport, Illinois, hosted a conference for its human resource people from all over the country, there was a mystery game the night before the conference started. Each guest was given a character to play and the background and attributes of that character. As the story unfolded, the characters had to interact with each other to solve the mystery. People met each other, and a good time was had by all.

A good example of how corporations can demonstrate their flexibility can be found at DataTel in Fairview, Virginia. The company's Director of Human Resources, Larry Lemmon, leaves early on Thursday afternoons to work with the youth at his church. The company knows about his dedication to these young people and enthusiastically supports Lemmon's work for his church. Lemmon makes up the hours at different times during the workweek.

volved in the process. Some workers will want to work established hours every day, different from when most people work. Others will want to vary their schedule every day, as long as they get their work done. Another group will want a set schedule, but will want to be able to vary from that schedule if someone close to them is sick, if a child is in a play at school, if that employee has an appointment during normal working hours, or has some personal work to do.

Moreover, the flexibility that employees are looking for does not come with strings attached. Employees do not want to be denigrated or punished for requesting this flexibility. The culture must support its employees as whole persons with families, not just work machines.

Stimulate and Support Recognition

Research conducted for years confirms that people like to be appreciated. They want to be recognized for what they've accomplished. As Bob Nelson observes in *1001 Ways to Reward Employees*, the following guidelines will help you establish a program of recognition and reward.

1. Match the reward to the person. It's important to understand that different people value different things. One person's coveted reward may seem ho-hum to another. By matching the reward to the person, you avoid rewarding with something of low perceived value, that might even have the opposite of the intended effect.

2. Match the reward to the achievement. An achievement attained over years should be rewarded differently than one realized after weeks or months of work. Rewards should be based on the amount of time you have to plan and implement them and your budget.

3. Be timely and specific. Rewarding an employee months after the worthy accomplishment or event is virtually meaningless. Reward as close in time to the achievement as possible. We give spot bonuses of cash on the spur of the moment. The recognition that goes along with the reward needs to acknowledge the employee for the *specific* success.[6]

Employers of Choice often have elaborate and well-designed programs of recognition and reward. It's common for companies to award Employees of the Week, Month or Year. But in addition to these old standards, Employers of Choice generally have their own company-specific programs, often well-entrenched and complete with acronyms that reinforce "on the team" feelings.

Involve Employees' Families

Practically all of the people working with you have support groups outside work. These support groups—families—are, of course, important to your employees. They want to spend time with them and to be closely connected with them. Sometimes, the desire to be with family conflicts with the need to get things done at work. This conflict can dissolve into an adversarial relationship between the employer and the family. In this kind of circumstance, the employer rarely wins.

Employers of Choice recognize the value of the family in the lives of their workers. They reach out to involve the family, building a cooperative three-sided relationship. Family events are recognized—birthdays, wedding anniversaries, graduations, and other occasions both happy and sad. Support is given when family

Microsoft's corporate culture can be characterized in one word—flexibility. Each employee works with his or her supervisor to establish working arrangements (hours and location). Supervisors focus on the results, not simply on hours in the chair.

Microsoft has also moved to greater flexibility in their perks. For example: instead of offering a one-day family event at the zoo, fortunate Microsoft employees may visit the zoo at a discounted rate with their families at any time during a designated period.

If you live in Kansas City, you've probably heard of a full-service public relations and communications firm called Blades & Associates. Blades shares year-end profits in a bonus distribution program.

New rewards and incentives are created almost monthly. For example, when the 16-person agency reached its $1 million revenue goal two months ahead of schedule, all celebrated with a three-fold reward that included

    a. team celebration of creativity—a pottery painting party

    b. personal celebration with a half-day to play "hooky"

    c. celebration with a significant person who supports the employee in his or her career with a $75 dining certificate at their favorite restaurant.[7]

The ACE (All Can Excel) Program inspires employees of Time Warner Communications, Columbus, Ohio. They nominate each other for the recognition—from a job well done to going beyond the call of duty. A committee assesses nominations and rewards points that recipients can redeem for Warner Bros. products such as jackets, mugs, and tee-shirts. ACE winners may also select American Express Gift Certificates. At the end of the year, Grand ACE Winners are selected to attend the annual incentive trip honoring star performers nationwide.[8]

---

members are ill or have passed away. Practices range from sending flowers when someone is ill or has died to providing gifts—sometimes scholarships—when an employee's child graduates from high school or college. Parties which include employees' families can also be quite beneficial.

Sponsor events for families—including picnics, trips to amusement parks, and parties at work for Christmas, Halloween, and public service projects. If your company supports walks for charities, such as The March of Dimes or Muscular Dystrophy, invite employees' entire families to come along. Consider incentives like tee shirts for all or a pizza party afterwards.

Recognize and Include the Children

Children are special. Even though they are included when we do family things, there are a couple of special considerations you ought to think about. Welcome children at work when they're not in school, for instance on teacher workdays. Arrange for some activities that will be fun, safe, and perhaps educational. These activities can be based at the company facilities, such as movies or entertainment in the company auditorium. Or, the kids can go on company-supported or subsidized field trips to a local museum or zoo.

Many high schools schedule "shadow days," when students spend the day with a worker—perhaps a parent, perhaps not—to learn what that person does including what his or her job involves.

Invite employees to arrange shadow opportunities in your company. Offer co-op employment or summer jobs to children of employees as appropriate.

Promote Convenience

As workers' lives become more complicated, they seek more and more opportunities for convenience. Employers who make their employees' lives easier and more convenient will certainly be more attractive than companies that ignore this important aspect of people's lives. Some organizations are getting very creative in how they help their people manage life's routine.

Some larger companies are devoting significant sections of their buildings to space for dry cleaners, sundry stores, shoe repair, and company logo clothing.

Use Technology to Stay Connected with Your People

People feel disconnected unless you reach out deliberately to build relationships with them. This closeness wasn't a problem in the past, when most employees were located in one place and saw each other almost every day. As companies have grown and become more dispersed, staying in touch has become more of a challenge. It's particularly difficult with telecommuters and virtual employees.

To maintain the bonds with your people, reach out to them using the wonderful technology that's available to us today. Facsimile machines are ubiquitous in offices and homes, so sending

Emerson Electric in St. Louis has a big Christmas party—mostly for the children of their employees. This gala event, arranged by Dick Hall Productions, features face painters, fortune tellers, an interactive magician, and entertainers who sing children's songs. But the most fun activity for the children is cake decorating. The children love seeing their edible handiwork, and being able to take it home.[9]

HMOs and third party payor organizations traditionally have not been considered optimal places to work. That was before United Healthcare. The Greensboro, North Carolina, office provides some unusual benefits for its employees. At Halloween, not only do the employees dress up, but the employees' children come trick or treating in the office. The employees pay for the candy, and the company provides prizes for the best costumes. The company's CEO, Frank Mascia, sets the tone for the employee-centered culture. Not surprisingly, United Healthcare enjoys a relatively low turnover rate.[10]

regular faxes to your people can work. E-mail is efficient, practically cost-free, and easy to use. Intranets, extranets, corporate voicemail systems, and even post cards offer vehicles to stay connected. When people feel more a part of an organization, the chances of them choosing to stay are much greater than when they just get work done, but don't feel a part of something.

Every summer, Texas Instruments holds a camp for employees' children at its Dallas, Texas, headquarters fitness facility. The Summer Time Kids Camp, which started in 1995, served approximately 100 children, ages 5 to 11, in 1998. The 11-week program, which costs $100 per child per week, runs from 7 A.M. to 6 P.M., Monday through Friday, and provides hot lunches and weekly field trips for the children. The camp is operated by Bright Horizons Family Solutions, a national corporate childcare company.

Located in Charlotte, North Carolina, Wilton Conner Packaging has 0.5 percent turnover (not a misprint). We're not surprised. Although the company has only about 200 employees, it offers an extraordinary array of employee perks. You don't have transportation? No problem. The Wilton Conner vanpool will pick you up in the morning and drop you off in the evening. You don't like to do laundry? Bring your dirty laundry to work with you in the morning and take home clean laundry in the

Support Simplicity

Life is increasingly complicated. It's overly complicated, in fact. The complexity is confusing, bewildering, challenging, upsetting, irritating, and de-motivating. Very few people choose to be in a more complicated environment, but many will choose, if they have the opportunity, to be in a less complicated environment.

Attack complexity! Find ways to simplify processes, systems, rules and regulations, relationships. In recent years, city governments have examined their approval processes for the granting of building permits and have discovered dozens of steps that must be followed—often including a variety of forms in a variety of offices in different buildings! They've moved aggressively to make things much easier by removing and combining steps, streamlining forms and eliminating confusion and double work. Apply the same processes in your organization—challenge and question the way your processes work for both internal and external customers.

Make it easy to get things done, and don't forget to simplify the application process. A complicated application process will turn people off before you even get a chance to talk with them.

Make Vacation Time Mandatory to Avoid Burnout

There's so much to do. Things are happening so quickly. Everyone is needed all the time because there are never enough people to get everything done. In organizations that are described as Employers of Choice, workers are highly dedicated and responsible. They take "own" their work and find it difficult to get away for vacations.

This strong commitment is admirable, but also risky. Without balance—and a break once in a while—people can unwittingly push themselves into burnout. Minimize this problem by requiring people to use their vacation time. If things are really intense, you might even want to institute mandatory time off on a quarterly basis.

Stage Employee Appreciation Events

Another way to take a much-needed break is to stage employee appreciation events. They don't have to be huge productions; a relatively small activity will often do just fine. With these events, you can accomplish several worthwhile objectives: 1) you send a message that people are appreciated; 2) you give people a good excuse and method for taking a break; and 3) you give people another opportunity to just "be" with their co-workers.

evening. But Conner doesn't stop there. When the maintenance men are not fixing the machinery, they are at employees' homes fixing leaky faucets or handling other minor home repairs.[11]

In June 1998, IHS HelpDesk Services had a problem. It was experiencing more than 300 percent turnover and couldn't grow. New hires were quitting after one or two months, one or two days, or in some cases, not showing up at all. If the company was to survive, it needed to take action—and fast!

As it turns out, they were sending their analysts out to client sites with no connection to the company. The company realized it needed to stay in touch with its employees, no matter where they were located. Now, everyday on people's desks when they arrive for work, is a one-page fax, called Daily Helpings. The fax contains news about new software, birthdays, anniversaries, jokes, games, new training offered by the company, profiles of successful analysts, and stories from the analysts themselves.

The company also needed an early warning system to find out

about any employee dissatisfactions so that they might be corrected. The company instituted a program whereby someone from headquarters called each analyst at least every other week to check in and ask, "how things were going." The company's analysts were connected. The company's turnover dropped to about 25 percent and is now at about 18 percent. Creating these connections is not the whole story, but connections played a major role in reducing the turnover rate.[12]

Encourage Creative Breaks

Research by the National Sleep Foundation in Washington, D.C., has shown that at least 37 percent of the population becomes so sleepy during the day that it interferes with daily activities, and the number increases to 52 percent for shift workers. In surveys, workers who acknowledged daytime sleepiness self-reported that job performance decreased by 30 percent.[15]

Some employers have responded to employee sleepiness problems with a disciplinary approach. They remove lids from toilets so workers can't lean back on them and sleep. They install bright lights in

---

Nordstrom is famous for the simplicity of its employee handbook. In fact, below is the Nordstrom Employee Handbook, in its entirety!

WELCOME TO NORDSTROM

We're glad to have you with our Company.

Our number one goal is to provide outstanding customer service.

Set both your personal and professional goals high.

We have great confidence in your ability to achieve them.

Nordstrom Rules:

Rule #1: Use your good judgment in all situations.

There will be no additional rules.

Please feel free to ask your department manager, store manager or division manager any question at any time.

Think about the messages that this simplicity sends to employees: "We trust you." "We know we can depend on you to do the right thing." "You are empowered to get the job done." And finally, "We're here to support you in doing that job—when and if you need us."

Does it work? You bet it does. In 1999, Nordstrom was named one of the 100 Best Companies to Work for in America.[13] And the company was named the tenth-best company to work for by Working Woman Magazine.[14]

break rooms so employees can't put their heads down on a table for a quick nap.

There's a better way. Recognize that human beings do get drowsy, especially when they've been engaged in repetitive or boring work. Solution: get creative with break times. Encourage people to take a power nap—at their desks or in a special room with low lighting and couches and soft chairs. Include timers or alarm clocks so people can easily manage the brevity of their rest. Physical activity can also wake people up and re-energize them. Some companies are even sponsoring scheduled recesses with intramural games.

Vacations can be a huge bonus. Take, for example, Motek, the software company in Beverly Hills, California. CEO Ann Price gives each of her employees one month off per year—with pay. Price also gives each employee $5,000, but there is a catch. That $5,000 must be used for airlines, cruises, hotels, and other travel expenses. Employees are expected to use time off to rest and rejuvenate.

Recognize Special Occasions and Milestones

Everyone has days that are important to them, for one reason or another. They like to at least acknowledge the day, and many people like to really celebrate. Each person has a different attitude about how special occasions are recognized, so this is not a one-size-fits-all proposition.

Birthdays are celebrated by everyone—sometimes with great fanfare, sometimes quietly. Before organizing a gala party, understand the celebrant's preferences. Our research has shown that birthdays are celebrated, in one way or another, in most workplaces. Methods include presentation of gag gifts, decorating the celebrant's

Stanley Furniture, in Stanleytown, Virginia, was proud of the work done by employees to raise funds that supported the Henry County-Martinsville United Way. When the campaign was complete, the company sponsored a picnic during a lunch hour. On that day administrative employees left their offices and walked out to the parking lot where a buffet lunch was waiting for them. After everyone enjoyed a delicious meal, the vice president of human resources and the local United Way campaign chairman thanked everyone and recognized the leaders of the effort. After the refreshing break, everyone returned to work, well-fed, appreciated, and energized. Similar events are held for the company's production workforce in its plants.

work area, cake (often decorated) and ice cream, a pizza party, an after-work party, going out to lunch with co-workers or a pot-luck lunch. An increasing number of senior executives are sending greeting cards to the employee's home and some companies even give the employee a day off during the birthday week.

Anniversaries of employment are celebrated in some companies. Some of the same methods used for birthdays apply in this case. In addition, there may be an anniversary "year pin" from the employer, and perhaps some sort of gift or bonus.

Other occasions worthy of celebration include meeting goals, winning an important contract, winning industry awards or reaching another milestone in the company's history.

Practice Aggressive Internal Marketing

Employers of Choice are constantly reinforcing their internal brand identities through consistent internal marketing. Each and every piece of internal correspondence, electronic or paper, is congruent with the corporate messages of the importance of individuals' contributions, corporate caring for its employees, and customer focus.

From job postings to house organs to announcements of corporate events, they are all written in

---

Gymboree, located in Burlingame, California designs, manufactures and retails a complete line of children's fashion apparel, accessories, and play products. They market those products exclusively through their own nearly 500 corporate-owned and managed stores in the United States, Canada, and the United Kingdom. In addition, the company operates/franchises more than 400 interactive parent/child play programs worldwide.

About a year ago, Gymboree began a once-a-week program of "corporate recess." Every Thursday at 3 P.M., a bell sounds over the public address system. Recess lasts for 20 minutes. Gymboree's campus sports a lake with a walking area, and hopscotch is available. The purpose of recess is to spend a few minutes together outside of the work environment catching up with one another, getting some fresh air and exercise, and creating a sense of team.

Each Wednesday at 3 P.M., Gymboree also provides snack time for its employees. This break lasts for about 20 minutes, during which time workers gather in a central location to munch on the snacks that include chips and salsa and cookies and milk.

These two corporate benefits reflect the Gymboree's "celebrate childhood" philosophy and are only two of the myriad family-friendly benefits the company offers.[16]

language that makes employees *want to* read them. That language focuses on the benefits to employees and not just the features. It's written in a style that answers the readers' main question: "What's in it for me?"

Employers of Choice have newsletters that highlight and picture the accomplishments of individuals and departments for all to see. Sometimes graphs reflect the achievements; other times a picture is worth a thousand words. These employers know the power of acknowledgment and offer tribute to their high achievers.

Remember Your Alumni

We're watching a trend in which people return to employers they left—after a period of years, months, weeks, or even days. These returning workers are called "boomerang employees." The stigma of going back where you were has all but disappeared, but many employees still don't return. Why not? They haven't been invited!

Stay in touch with your alumni. Send them company newsletters, e-mail greetings, or birthday cards. Remember what aspects of your work excited them, then let them know about what's

Camet Corporation in Hiram, Ohio, has a monthly party for all employees who have birthdays in that month and those who have anniversary dates of employment during the same period. The company shuts down during the celebration time, about 20–30 minutes, while all the employees join together for cake and coffee, and punch or soft drinks. The company president offers a few words of congratulations and gives a quick report on corporate achievements. Who answers the telephones during this period? Retirees, who welcome an opportunity to come in once a month to visit with old friends.

Business Stationery, Inc., Cleveland, Ohio, was challenged by a high level of re-work. Recognizing that all the jobs that had to be done over were costing the company a lot of money, the managers decided to attack the problem head-on, with an incentive. They persuaded the company president to cook Easter breakfast for all employees on Good Friday if they met their goal. Then, they sweetened the deal by getting him to agree to wear a bunny suit while he cooked, if they reached a stretch goal.

Long story, short: the company president, Frank Spontelli, Jr., looked adorable in his bunny suit as he cooked breakfast for three shifts. Bonus: Frank worked as a short order cook in college, so the meals were well-prepared and delicious!

happening in those areas of your company. They might want to come back and become involved with those efforts again. Remember that people are changing jobs much more frequently now. In today's workplace, it seems like the right thing to do. Sometimes people jump the fence to go to where the grass is greener—only to discover that it's crab grass. They've made a mistake, but are they allowed to go back to where they were? If you'd like to have them back, tell them.

One company that has an interesting approach to Internal Marketing is the software cataloger, SoftChoice. This company wins employee accolades with its "virtual community center."

Located in Toronto, Canada, SoftChoice has a newsletter on their Intranet. Intranet technology gives them the resources to make the project a living document that reflects input not from a single editor, but from any employee who wants to contribute.

The SoftChoice Interactive Newsletter, or Sinews, as it came to be called, is more than a newsletter. Just as its name suggests, Sinews functions as the connective tissue in the organization. It's a community center with different departments containing articles that reflect news, such as the status of new branch openings, and forums for sharing best practices. As people lose interest in different topics, they disappear and are replaced by new departments.

When employees visit Sinews, they are encouraged to submit articles on any topic, post responses to existing topics, or e-mail the writer directly. New material is cycled through a minimal review process that addresses spelling, grammar, and punctuation issues. No one ever heavily edits the articles. Sinews gives literally every employee a voice to engage in public discourse on anything and everything.

Besides providing a valuable channel for proposing new ideas and sharing best practices, Sinews gives people the freedom to inform, commend, and criticize. This freedom enables SoftChoice to take full advantage of the creative minds it has in the organization. Because the idea for Sinews came out of such a dialogue—and because it fosters so many more dialogues—it truly reflects the innovation companies can achieve by understanding and promoting their corporate culture. The bottom line is workforce stability—in an organization with 247 employees located in 27 offices throughout North America, their turnover is only 6.1%.[17]

Some of the more enlightened companies, notably J.P. Morgan, even have alumni associations of people who used to work for their company. The company sponsors annual events for their former employees. Other companies even invite the former employees join in celebrations with their current employees. And guess what happens? Not surprisingly, some of those former employees choose to return to their previous employers.[18]

Notes

1. *Lean & Meaningful*, pp. 74–76, by Roger Herman and Joyce Gioia, Oakhill Press, 1998.
2. "Cheesecake Factory turns non-employees into recruiters," by Roger Herman, *The Workforce Stability Alert*, February 1999, p. 3.
3. Interview with Bob Noble, December 17, 1999.
4. *Lean & Meaningful*, pp. 208–209, by Roger Herman and Joyce Gioia, Oakhill Press, 1998.
5. Interview with Dick Hall, December 16, 1999.
6. *1001 Ways to Reward Employees*, xv–xvi, by Bob Nelson, Workman Press, 1994.
7. "Small company offering big benefits—Blades & Associates," *The Workforce Stability Alert*, October 1999, p. 4.
8. Jeanie Casison, *Incentive* Magazine, April 1999, p. 46.
9. Interview with Dick Hall, December 16, 1999.
10. "Celebrate with Children," by Joyce Gioia, *The Workforce Stability Alert*, August 1998, p.5.
11. "Diligent Caring Yields 0.5 percent Turnover," by Roger Herman, *The Workforce Stability Alert*, October 1998, p. 3.
12. "How You Gonna Keep 'Em Down on the Firm?" by Chris Caggiano, *Inc.* Magazine, January 1998, p. 75.
13. *The 100 Best Companies to Work for in America*, by Robert Levering and Milton Moskowitz, Penguin Books, 1999, pp. 327–332.
14. "Top Companies for Executive Women," *Working Women* Magazine, January 2000, p. 52.
15. "Sleep on This," Anita Bruzzese, *Human Resource Executive*, May 19, 1998.
16. "Too stressed-out to work" Enjoy recess and snack times when you work for Gymboree," by Joyce Gioia, *The Workforce Stability Alert*, August 1999.
17. "SoftChoice wins accolades with virtual 'community center,'" *The Workforce Stability Alert*, February 1999, p. 2.
18. "Employees reunite to chew fat, talk jobs," by Stephanie Armour, *USA Today*, July 9, 1999, p. 14B.

GROWTH AND OPPORTUNITY

Our strong economy has created a wide range of exciting, attractive jobs in many fields throughout the country. This plethora of opportunities will exist for years to come. Workers know they will have plenty of places to go, but they will have to be prepared to do the job required to have the best chance of being hired.

Whether they expect to change jobs within the same employer or go to a different company, these astute workers want to be as marketable as possible. To maintain their marketability, they must keep their skills sharp and pick up new skills and knowledge whenever possible. They want training. They want development opportunities. They want new challenges. They want mentoring and coaching.

Today's employees are more aggressive in their drive for ongoing learning and growth. Expect them to make these issues factors in their employment agreements. They want learning opportunities at work and/or they want reimbursement of their tuition, fees, and other costs of attending a nearby college or university. The interest will be in both academic courses and continuing education offerings.

PEOPLE WANT TO LEARN AND GROW

Employers of Choice recognize their people's burning desire to acquire knowledge and skill. They create and maintain a learning environment to respond to employee interest and to manifest the employer's dedication to employee growth and development. Time off for training courses or to attend a college class will be commonplace, usually with ways for the employees to make up the time by working longer hours or by doing special assignments.

Supervisors at all levels must encourage learning. Each performance appraisal interview should include a discussion of the next steps in the employee's development. A plan for the next period will be discussed and designed. This next-term plan will fit into the employee's long-term growth plan. Every employee—from the CEO to the custodian to the newest hire—will have a personal growth plan. Each plan will be different, of course, reflecting the type and degree of training to be accomplished.

Management people need training, development, and feedback to support their professional growth. While many companies invest heavily in educating middle managers and enhancing their skills, there is much more to be done. This circumstance is especially prevalent today, as corporate cultures and work environments undergo rapid change.

A number of employers have formed corporate universities to train and educate their people. The American Society for Training and Development describes this arena as the fastest growing segment of the adult education field. It is estimated that there are more than 1600 corporate universities today, as compared to 400 in 1998. At the current rate, the number of corporate universities could surpass the number of traditional universities by 2010. Corporate universities could become the primary educators of post-secondary students in the

---

At Baptist Hospital, Inc., Pensacola, Florida, cultural change was essential. Admissions were flat and patient satisfaction measured by a national survey was slightly below average. As part of the turnaround, the hospital made an investment in middle management development. Now, all of their leaders—nurse managers, supervisors, and department heads—go off-site for two days every 90 days. Employee forums are held every 90 days and employees are surveyed about their attitudes toward their supervisors. The leaders get "report cards" every three months to check behavior and performance against goals. The critical goals are customer service, efficiency, expense management, and employee turnover. Vice presidents are measured using the same criteria, and 20 percent of executive incentive compensation is based on employee turnover.[1]

United States. "Another reason for the rise of corporate universities is the desire of many companies to be perceived as the Employer of Choice in their industries. Consequently, they are using their investment in employee education—especially in a corporate university—as evidence of their competitive advantage for recruiting and retaining the best and brightest employees."[2]

In some organizations, emphasis is placed on educating management and/or salespeople. In others, courses are available for everyone. There are many different designs, including relationships with universities and colleges to enhance instructor quality and availability, curriculum design, and academic credit. In the late 1980s, our consulting firm designed, developed, and operated a corporate university for Meridia Healthcare System in the Cleveland, Ohio, area. As part of the program, we arranged for academic credit to be granted by a local private college.

A versatile library of learning materials including books, magazines and journals, audiotapes, videotapes, self-study courses, and computer-based instructional tools will enhance this learning environment. These materials should be available for check-out by any employee at any time. Many companies enjoy inter-library loan arrangements with local public library systems, essentially making *any* resource from the library available to employees.

Accomplishments in training and development need to be recognized, in most cases with a framable or framed certifi-

---

Motorola, Inc., founded its corporate university in 1981. Motorola University, a free-standing educational division of the company, offers training in cutting-edge industry disciplines, business skills, and a sprinkling of liberal arts courses—such as foreign languages—that enhance job skills on a global level. Operating from its headquarters in Schaumburg, Illinois, Motorola University now has nearly 1,300 full- and part-time teachers in 20 countries where Motorola people work. See more of what this pioneer is doing by visiting www.motorola.com.[3]

"Thomson Corporation, a $6 billion information and publishing company, wants to be the Employer of Choice in its industry. It will do that by sending its 8,000 people back to school for courses in basic computing, software development, leadership and change management appropriately called 'Life in the Fast Lane.'"[4]

Thomson University (TU), created in 1996, offers on-site education, satellite training centers, distance learning, and video conferencing, from its campus in Eagan, Minnesota. Virtually all of Thomson's employees have taken courses. In addition to all classrooms being equipped with satellite down-links, TU has a full library for employee use. The curriculum includes formal classes, personal coaching, and practical classes in such topics as personal finance for first-time home-buyers. The employee turnover rate at Thomson is half the industry average; the company's commitment to education is seen as a key factor.

At Lucent Technologies, the goal is 15 days of training per employee each year. Its Learning and Performance Center is located at the company's New Jersey headquarters. Having evolved from a basic skills curriculum, employees are now expected to take individual responsibility for their own learning and education.[5]

Dell University, SunU, and Veri-fone University have no campus at all; they've committed to the virtual university model.[6] Dell offers 70 percent of its courses in virtual mode. Sprint University of

cate of achievement mounted on the recipient's office or cubicle wall, or in a suitable place near the employee's workstation.

In what ways, *specifically*, can Employers of Choice work to foster this environment of growth and opportunity?

Concentrate on Individuals

As the result of management and leadership styles applied in most organizations over the past decade, there is a tendency to interact with employees as teams and as work groups. While this kind of relationship has its place, Employers of Choice need to focus on relating to employees as individuals.

Today's workers are relatively independent. They want to be recognized as individuals, unique in their own right. They expect to be treated specially, even though you're also treating other employees as special individuals. In the learning arena, this expectation means that supervisors, managers, and executives should seek ways to develop each individual employee differently in order to maintain that sense of being unique, special, and distinct.

Utilize Individual Growth Plans

Create a growth plan for each employee at the time of hiring. In some cases, you may even want to begin a sketch of the plan during the hiring/interview process as part of the recruiting effort. The employee gets a copy of this plan, which will change over time, and so does the employee's supervisor. Of course, a copy goes in the employee's personnel file. If your company has a training department, those professionals should also be involved in the plan development at some point and probably should have a copy of at least part of the plan.

The individual growth plan is an ever-changing document. It gets updated as people complete training, as they make career shifts, and need or desire a different set of knowledge and skills. It can also change as new learning opportunities become available. The plan is reviewed and adjusted each time an employee is formally reviewed as part of the performance appraisal process. It's a living document.

Include a variety of learning experiences in each employee's plan, not just items such as, "Will attend company training on . . . " As you develop the unique plan for each person, consider special assignments, coaching, mentoring, college or university courses, seminars offered by industry trade associations, or commercial seminars. Cross-training and cross-experience may fit, as well.

Coaching, once used principally for fast trackers, is becoming much more prevalent in corporate America. A 1999 study of 488 human resource professionals, by Lee Hecht Harrison, reported that 70 percent of employers used coaching for leadership development, 64 percent for skill development or style differences, and 40 percent to retain top talent. Fast trackers received most of the attention in 26 percent of the companies, but 54 percent said they provided coaching equally to high potential and other employees.

Excellence has 50 percent of its 1000 courses available through videos, workbooks, the World Wide Web, and the company intranet. The company is moving to put everything except management and professional development on the intranet. Sprint's research shows that students learned only slightly more by computer than in the classroom, but they gained the knowledge in just over half the time. With the tight demand for people to be on-the-job, reducing the students' time away from work is a major benefit.[7]

A small municipal police department in Ohio had framed certificates of completion of a wide range of training on the department's lobby wall. The floor-to-ceiling display showcased a row of certificates for each of the officers in the department. Officers could change which of their certificates would be on display at any time.

The growth in coaching, according to the survey, is coming from the benefits of helping people improve instead of replacing them according to 60 percent of respondents. Fifty-four percent responded that good talent is harder to find and retain.[8]

Develop your coaching plan collaboratively with the employee. It's a team effort. The plan should concentrate on what learning and training the employee wants, as well as what's good for the employer. Show anticipated (approximate or specific) dates when the training might be scheduled. Some of the experiences will take place over the next six months to a year; others may be further out. When the employee sees that learning will be an ongoing process—for years—there will be a greater tendency for the workers to remain longer with the employer.

Emphasize Supervisor's Developmental Role

Although each employee works for the organization in the larger sense, the closest work relationship is between the worker and his or her immediate supervisor. This relationship is vitally important: it is the key connection that influences how the worker feels about the organization, the workgroup, the work to be done, potential growth, and future opportunities. The unfortunate shortcoming is that these front-line supervisors have not been sufficiently trained, educated, and prepared to care for their people.

The front-line supervisor has a vital role to play in the development of his or her people. As the representative of the employer who is closest to the worker, the supervisor has the greatest understanding of who the employee is, what opportunities may lie ahead, and what training and development might be needed to position the employee for promotion.

In addition to arranging formal training classes for workers, the supervisor works closely with each employee on a one-to-one basis. There are all sorts of on-the-job learning opportunities. Good supervisors stay alert for those occasions when little things can be taught. Gaining that on-the-spot knowledge gives workers confidence and a greater sense of partnership with the supervisor and employer.

Supervisors should maintain open lines of communication with the human resources department and with the training department. There should be a high awareness of the training programs available—both now and in the future. This knowledge of things to come should be factored into the planning and growth relationship between supervisors and employees. Reversing the communication flow, supervisors should keep human resource and training professionals abreast of employee development needs so that these staff specialists can support them with the development of new training and education programs.

How Much Is Enough?

There is a wide range of thought about how much training and development time is enough. Results and a sense of growth are difficult to measure. It's a feeling that the employee, the supervisor, and other leaders have to sense. One measure has been the number of hours of classroom time invested each year. We've seen that number as low as zero formal hours to as high as 120 hours per year. A comfortable standard seems to be about 40 hours per year of classroom "seat time," whether that's in sessions delivered by the employer or by outside organizations.

It's important to note here that seat time doesn't necessarily produce growth and productivity results. The core issue is what learning takes place and, often more importantly, the application of the new learning. To achieve legitimate application of the learning, the employee's supervisors and colleagues must provide opportunities for the worker to discuss what has been learned, to seek appropriate avenues for application, to use the knowledge or skills, then to evaluate how well the learning helped the employee perform. This extended process will serve as a better indicator of the value of the learning.

Advocate Mentoring

People who are fortunate enough to work for Employers of Choice enjoy and benefit from the mentoring they receive—formally and informally—as part of their employment. From a position of relative obscurity a few years ago, mentoring has moved to center stage as a means to help people grow and advance in their careers.

Formal mentoring programs have been established in some companies. Employees and mentors, usually within the organization, are assigned to work with each other. A central office of mentoring, or at least an employee or two charged with administrating the process, sets up the official relationship and monitors meetings, progress, and results. Our experience suggests that such formal mentoring programs can actually be counterproductive and should not be selected as the optimal approach. Force-fitting mentors and protégés creates uncomfortable conditions for both participants in the process.

Mentoring can be encouraged and facilitated, though, on an informal basis by the employer. There are several things that can be done to help employees benefit from the wisdom, experience, and counseling of others who have been there and done that. Each of these efforts is designed to help people voluntarily experience the process of mentorship, without forcing anyone to participate. When actions are voluntary, they're usually more successful.

Establish a registry of people interested in serving as mentors. The obvious prospects are experienced (and stereotypically older) executives, managers, salespeople, and master craftsmen. Appreciating that we can learn from people who are our peers or who are younger than we are, expand that list to include, for instance, young employees who know a lot more about how to use computers than senior executives do.

Invite those interested in mentoring to sign up using a paper form, an intranet form, or some other means. Ask them to provide information such as their education, experience, and how many protégés they're willing to mentor. If they have any preferences regarding what they'd like to concentrate on in the mentoring relationship, that's valuable information to collect. For instance, a senior executive may have a considerably broad background, but may want to concentrate on mentoring people interested in global careers or in manufacturing.

Make this list of available mentors available for access by employees interested in mentors. An ideal format would be a searchable database on a company intranet. Another alternative would be a three-ring notebook with a page for each mentor, perhaps with a cross index. Those people interested in finding one or more mentors could consult the registry and determine whom they feel might be most appropriate for their personality and for what they seek from the mentoring experience.

Under this design, the person seeking a mentor contacts the prospective mentor, arranges an appointment, and conducts an interview. If, after their interview, the two of them decide to enter into a mentoring relationship, the mentor should advise the registry custodian. Notification keeps the list of who is available current.

For example, if the vice president of finance offers to mentor two people and one relationship is established, the registry should show that only one more opportunity is currently available. When a second protégé is acquired, the registry will show that the vice president is serving as a mentor, but is not accepting new protégés at this time. If and when one of those mentoring relationships ends, the vice president could again make himself or herself available for another relationship.

Another approach is to simply encourage mentoring, asking employees to be receptive to inquiries from others. Then invite all employees to approach members of the organization whom

Trevira, a Hoechst Celanese division that develops polyester fibers in North Carolina and South Carolina, discovered "a large [knowledge] gap between expected retirees and a strong group of engineers who had been with the firm less than 10 years. The company developed a year-long mentoring program that includes several elements. The key piece is a learning group that's made up of five or six mentees and a mentor. The group members, not the mentor, control both the meeting times and the frequency. The mentor provides perspective and insight on the corporation's culture, politics, and how decisions get made and why.

HR designed the groups, looking for diversity in race, gender, educational background, and experience in the organization. The mentors, also called "learning leaders," were assigned, as well. Once assembled, the groups had to work out any problems themselves. The program has produced the desired results so far. Graduates of the program are progressing into leadership roles within the company. Management support has also been considerable and mentees are encouraged to meet with executives for informational interviews.[9]

they think can be effective mentors and invite those members to become mentors. No corporate intervention is necessary; the relationship develops informally and unofficially.

Bank of America began seriously considering mentoring after several talented, high-potential minority employees left the bank. Management realized that if these people had built more relationships with senior management, they might not have felt that leaving was their only alternative. Brian Smith, vice president of personnel in Dallas, Texas, observed that "minorities often feel they don't have allies who can show them how things work and where to get help."

In response, the bank established a mentoring program. Most of the 20 mentors are white males; the 40 mentees are mostly minorities. This diverse pairing challenges members of both groups to venture outside their comfort zones, Smith notes. The program offers one-on-one and group activities, including community discussion groups in which banking staff can explore both cross-cultural and cross-functional issues.[10]

Offer Basic Education and Training

The increasing prevalence of quality initiatives, the use of computers and other processes that require literacy and numeracy skills have revealed that a significant proportion of workers lack fundamental knowledge. Basic reading, writing, and arithmetic skills eluded many students during their growing years and, for quite a while, schools were passing these students from grade to grade. Eventually these students graduated to make their way in the real world. These unfortunate students were not adequately prepared; they didn't possess the reading, writing, and calculating skills that are so essential to success in today's more sophisticated world of work.

The most recent National Adult Literacy Survey by the National Center of Educational Statistics, U.S. Department of Education, showed that 21 percent of the U.S. adult population—40 million Americans over the age of 16—have only rudimentary reading and writing skills. Most adults in this category cannot write a letter explaining an error on their credit card bill. The same study revealed that the highest level of math skills for 22 percent of adults is simple arithmetic.

The National Institute for Literacy (NIFL) says American businesses lose more than $60 billion in productivity each year due to employees' lack of basic skills. Only 26 percent of companies offer training in basic written communication, even though 71 percent of executives surveyed by NIFL said the need was critical. Math skills are also deficient: 47 percent of the executives reported need for improvement, but only 5 percent of companies offered the training.[11] The problem is becoming more acute during the labor shortage as we reach into non-traditional labor pools where people may never have acquired the literacy and numeracy skills they need to get a decent job.

Many employers have arranged classes and have hired instructors—sometimes employees who volunteer to help—to educate employees who lack the knowledge they need to survive and thrive in the more challenging work environments of today and tomorrow. The motivation here is to take care of your own—to make a deeper investment in those good people who want to work with you, who want to succeed.

If you don't have enough participants or resources to make this kind of an effort efficient in your organization, talk with nearby employers about creating some sort of cooperative arrangement to hold classes. Coordinate with local schools or community colleges to learn how they can help and to discover what programs may already exist. Don't overlook community colleges; part of their mission is to help employers upgrade the capacity of the workforce.

The advice of the experts in this field is that class attendance should be voluntary. Incentives for participation and achievement, such as bonuses or wage increases and promotions might be appropriate. By

Ames Rubber, in Hamburg, New Jersey, initiated a new quality management program in 1987 and discovered a serious problem: Their people didn't have the reading, writing, and math skills to participate in everyday work. Ames required their entire workforce to take a reading and math test at the same time—everyone from the CEO to the janitor took the test at the same time, in the same environment. Of the 400 employees who took the test, 185 had skills in fourth- to sixth-grade levels.

To address the problem, Ames partnered with a local community college to develop a comprehensive training program in basic skills and English as a Second Language (ESL). Funding from the New Jersey Department of Labor paid the costs for materials and community college instructors; Ames paid for the employees' wages during class time. Classes were held once a week for 13 weeks. Those who needed further training were enrolled for another 13 weeks. The ESL classes are ongoing one-on-one tutoring sessions.

paying workers to attend classes, you emphasize the importance of training and your investment in your people. Another alternative is paying for half the time and holding the classes during nonwork time: both the employer and the employee are contributing and making a commitment. This approach also keeps people on the job when they're needed and avoids resentment from other employees about carrying the load while students are away. Make the process positive—people are growing through the acquisition of new skills—rather than negative, that is, that there's something wrong or deficient.

As you hire more workers from the welfare rolls or with other disadvantages, you'll discover more opportunities to substantially increase the knowledge, skills, capacity, and potential of current and future employees. Helping people become more productive and more attractive as employees—and as citizens—can be exceptionally rewarding. Include in your exploration an investigation about how you can help non-graduates earn their General Equivalency Diploma (GED). As employees increase their self-esteem, they increase their dedication and loyalty to you, their Employer of Choice.

Coaching can make a big difference for welfare-to-work employees. The corporate culture is foreign to them. For most supervisors, the cultural environment from which these workers come every day is beyond imagination. Volunteer mentors and coaches can be trained to know when they should help and when they should refer the worker to a professional counselor with the company's Employee Assistance Program.

Blue Cross-Blue Shield of Massachusetts offers three basic writing courses, one self-study and two group classes. Another class was scheduled to be added in January 2000.[12]

Xerox Corporation helps new workers through their voluntary Friends at Work program. Marriott International's Pathways to Independence program has hired more than 1,500 former welfare recipients and achieved a 65 percent retention rate among those workers. Marriott has found assigning a mentor and job shadowing for two-thirds of their six-week training to be effective. United Air Lines has achieved 50 percent retention with more than 1,000 welfare-to-work employees, but notes that the lower rate is not unusual for the airport industry because of varied work hours and the high proportion of part-time jobs.

Support Higher Education

The colleges and universities in your community are a tremendous resource. With a little support from their employers, thousands of workers are continuing in school or returning to earn a degree. Wise employers demonstrate their support of higher education in various ways, some of which directly involve their employees.

Tuition and fee reimbursement programs for employees have been around for a long time. Hundreds, if not thousands, of employers provide financial support for their workers. Payment is made for completion of a wide range of academic courses, even for some unrelated to the employee's work. The tendency now, particularly among companies that may be described as Employers of Choice, is to provide financial support for any courses the employee wishes to take, rather than insisting that the subject be consistent with the employee's present or future work. This liberal approach to repayment approval enables workers to continue their movement toward degrees that are broader or different than the work they're currently doing. It gives employees space for personal growth and personally managed growth.

Your business should strongly support continuing education programs by sending workers to seminars, and by inviting colleges to send instructors into the workplace. The breadth of courses available can be quite attractive for many employers and employees, and most colleges are willing to find and recruit instructors for desired courses that are not yet on their lists. Courses can be custom-designed on the continuing education

At Universal Studios Escape in Orlando, Florida, co-workers don't know that any given new employee has just come off the welfare rolls; that information is kept private and supervisors coach them, just as they coach all new employees. To address the inherent problems with former welfare recipients, Universal entered into a partnership with Lockheed Martin. Using a grant from the Central Florida Work and Gain Economic Self-Sufficiency Coalition, Universal hired a full-time, in-house job coach whose sole responsibility is to help welfare-to-work hires make that crucial transition. The grant also covers Lockheed's training expenses. The job coach writes vouchers for gasoline, bus tokens, and work apparel, and provides referrals to organizations that help with day care or other problems that may impede success.[13]

(non-academic) side of the house, responding directly to what employers need to strengthen and keep their people.

A substantial number of today's employees want to continue their education, regardless of what level they've already achieved. Even people with graduate degrees want further education. In our fast-moving world of work, keeping up with rapidly-changing technology and leadership techniques is essential for survival and continued marketability. Wise employers will endorse and encourage this drive from the time the employee is hired. By supporting personal and professional growth, you recognize the enhancement of the potential of each employee, something employees want to hear from their employer.

Encourage Skill Enhancement

Skills are built through training, rather than education. It's a different process, involving different techniques of instruction and learning. While education is usually provided by colleges and universities with some corporate involvement, training is usually primarily a corporate responsibility.

Ideally, the Employer of Choice has its own training department comprised of professional trainers with the expertise, skills, and experience necessary to assess training needs, to create and implement appropriate learning experiences, then to follow-up to ensure effective application of the new skills. Note the importance of follow-up. Simply delivering training and then dropping the learner in the lap of the

At CIGNA Group Insurance in Philadelphia, Pennsylvania, both employees and employer rank education at the top of the benefits list. There are two educational benefit programs. The Education Reimbursement Program is a nationwide effort that pays for employees who have completed undergraduate degrees to obtain advanced degrees.

The other program, more unusual, is the CIGNA-Penn program, through which employees can earn an undergraduate liberal arts degree from the University of Pennsylvania without leaving their workplace. Courses are taught by University faculty at company facilities. About 150 people are enrolled in the program, which is appreciated by employees who have minimal time and resources. The only expenses to the employee-students, who must meet university standards, are for application fees and books. Average per-employee cost to the company for a course is $850–900. Statistic: 97 percent of the graduates of the program have remained with the company.[14]

supervisor is not enough any more. Trainers working for Employers of Choice continue working with each of their learners, ensuring that skills are acquired sufficiently so they can be applied to achieve results. Their relationship with supervisors is one of partnership, enhancing the likelihood that the employee will use his or her new skills and that those skills will be reinforced by their immediate superiors.

Employers who don't have in-house training departments, for whatever reason—size, dispersed employees, cost—should still have someone assigned to ensure that all employees receive needed training on an ongoing basis. When trainers are not employed by the company, they should be hired as independent contractors to accomplish essentially the same objectives ascribed to in-house trainers.

Build Competence and Confidence

Employers of Choice invest significant resources in training employees to become more proficient in their jobs. As workers become more productive, they gain a new sense of confidence. This confidence, flowing from competence combined with experience, encourages workers to assume more responsibility and accountability, to take more initiative, and to seek ways to make improvements. Armed with this stronger linkage to the success of the organization, the employees' feeling of ownership and dedication is strengthened. Seeing greater results and feeling a sense of satisfaction, employees are more loyal, resulting in a long-term, mutually-beneficial relationship. The investment in training can reap tremendous rewards.

Provide Cross-Training

Many employers have a tendency to train workers to perform one job or one family of jobs. While this approach enables the employee to be a specialist, it also limits the employees' opportunities for growth and to make a contribution. This narrow focus limits how valuable the workers can be to the employer.

Cross-training and cross-experience in a number of different jobs enables an employee to better understand a number of aspects of the organization. Blinders and limits are lifted, enabling the worker to gain a helpful larger sense of what's happening— the "big picture." It's a lot easier for an employee to be loyal and dedicated to an organization when the larger perspective is in focus. The increased competence allows the employee to feel more a part of the larger organization, better able to make a significant contribution.

Ruth's Chris Steak House, a chain of upscale restaurants based in Metairie, Louisiana, hires very carefully, according to Shanna Lucien-White, Director of Human Resources. Everyone is expected to grow. Every employee must be certified and trained in a new position every month. Compensation is competency-based. Training, using self-managed "audio cards," is offered in Spanish and English.

The employer benefits from the cross-training and cross-experience as well. Now the employee better understands how other jobs relate to the primary assignment, so the work performed on the primary assignment may well be at a higher caliber. In addition, the worker can now fill in on an as-needed basis to perform other jobs when the workload is heavy or when someone else is not available—if a co-worker is ill or on vacation, perhaps.

Some companies shift workers several times a day to different jobs, giving them more variety in their work. When applied in manufacturing jobs, this practice can improve safety. The workers are less likely to get bored with repetitive work, reducing the likelihood of an accident. Workers who don't want to do the same job day in and day out welcome the variety. This job-changing approach can also be valuable in situations where more people are needed in different job functions at different times of the day.

OFFER A WIDE RANGE OF GROWTH OPPORTUNITIES

Training and education are important components of growth, but there are more options to consider. Special assignments, opportunities to teach others, involvement in decision-making, giving tours to visitors, and participation in quality teams or project teams all contribute to a worker's learning.

When developing the individualized growth plan for each employee, think expansively and creatively about how and what people can learn. Giving them books to read, tapes to listen to, or CD-ROMs to use can help people grow. Access to intranet or Internet research, learning, or even "surfing" can be productive. Participation in meetings and other activities in trade, commercial, professional, or community organizations can provide an invaluable learning experience.

Support Employee Involvement in Volunteer Groups

Corporate support of volunteer organizations is recognized as good community service and involvement. In this context, we acknowledge that when people are actively involved in volunteer organizations, of practically any sort, they have opportunities to build their leadership and management skills, to develop greater proficiency in collaboration and teamwork, and to gain a greater appreciation of how their personal contributions can help the group achieve.

Some of this volunteer work may require some occasional time-off from work. While the employees' absences may incur a temporary hardship, the lessons learned will be worth it. In voluntary organizations, members act of their own volition; they don't have to do what others in the organization tell them to do. They perform tasks because they want to. The experience of working with others who don't have to do what they're told provides a wonderful laboratory for learning how to inspire people to perform on their own initiative. When discipline, regulations, and obedient behavior aren't required, there's a totally different dynamic of how people work together.

Facilitate Worker Participation
in the Military Reserve or National Guard

Employees who serve in the military reserves or National Guard organizations also learn different skills—people skills and technical skills, among others. In these structured, relatively autocratic organizations, people are expected to do exactly as they are told. The experiences of military life, even on a part-time basis, provide stronger understandings of the need for discipline, order, and procedures. The sense of organization, of people working together, is quite valuable for people in business.

While many workers don't want to be ordered to do things, this leadership style is appropriate for many situations. The major key here, we believe, is the sense of discipline, orderliness, and working within a system to get things done.

Realistically, a business environment is a mixture of the need for consistency and discipline—and the need for individuality and flexibility. Achieving that balance is essential to an organization's success.

Promote from Within

When you promote from within, you send a clear, strong signal that your employees have talent, ability, experience, and the right to be promoted from within the organization. If you continually go outside the organization to recruit managers, you send a message to your people that they are not worthy. This perception seriously dampens their enthusiasm to develop and perform at a high level.

Sometimes people who work for you have done a fine job and are worthy of recognition. Don't promote them solely to recognize them for being good employees. Ensure that they are capable of doing the work that the new position requires, or you could be setting them up for failure. Employers of Choice provide pre-promotion training for many people moving into new jobs, acquainting them with their new responsibilities, and equipping them with the skills they'll need in their new roles. Mentoring can play a key role here, as well.

Employers of Choice provide alternative promotion routes for technicians, professionals, and others who deserve to be moved to positions of greater responsibility, status, and/or income, but who shouldn't—for one reason or another—be moved into (higher) management positions. Titles such as senior technician, lead engineer or master salesman could be used for such positions.

Arrange Lateral Transfers for Growth

As people grow, it's often appropriate to move them into positions where they can gain new or expanded experiences. These job shifts don't have to be up the corporate hierarchy. They may be lateral transfers.

Some lateral movements will be within the same department, perhaps to a companion position with somewhat different responsibilities. Some transfers may be to other departments or even other locations where employees will gain new knowledge, experience, and perspective. The transfers do not necessarily have to include any adjustments in compensation.

Depending on a variety of circumstances, it may be wise to frame these lateral transfers as special assignments. Military organizations have done this kind of transfer for decades, calling it Temporary Duty (TDY). The same kind of temporary assignment can apply in the business world.

Move Beyond Job Descriptions

For years, job descriptions were considered an essential aspect of employment. These documents were descriptive, but they have also been limiting in their scope. Position incumbents were told that certain duties were their responsibility, with the implication that other duties were not. In spite of the often-cited "other duties as assigned" phrase, the reality was that broader responsibilities rarely appeared.

In different times, the job description was an appropriate tool. The statement delineated roles clearly and supported the traditional bureaucratic model of workforce organization. However, things have changed. The job description is becoming obsolete.

Many organizations are replacing the job description with more broadly written role definitions that address competencies and mission more than specific tasks or tight responsibility areas. In the future, workers will assume a more wide-ranging set of responsibilities and accountabilities in a collaborative effort to accomplish organizational missions and objectives. Job descriptions will cease to be punitive, limiting, or controlling, shifting to a more open, encouraging depiction of what can be done.

Now might be a good time to begin an exploration of how this approach might work for you.

Encourage Young People and Support Public Education

These two components of becoming an Employer of Choice are closely linked. The growth and development of a productive, stable workforce includes efforts similar to farm teams in professional sports.

Astute employers look long-range in their strategic staffing work. They build their future by recruiting far in advance of need. In this regard, these employers hire high school students on a co-op basis during the school year, then employ them full-time during the summer. Students learn a considerable amount about business, gain insights into career opportunities, earn some money, and give employers a chance to groom them and evaluate their potential as permanent employees.

In addition to hiring students, these employers reach out to the schools through involvement in activities such as Junior Achievement or support of educational programs that are unique to particular schools or school districts.

The key here is not simply providing money for the schools, but becoming actively involved in working directly with students. The students learn, becoming more prepared and receptive to the idea of working for the companies involved. Early recruiting intertwines with training, growing young people to be fine future employees.

A few years ago, teachers and students at Copley High School in Copley, Ohio, a suburb of Akron, undertook an innovative and ambitious Moon Base project. Numerous corporations—local and national—provided funding and expertise for a year-long endeavor to teach students first-hand what it would be like to operate a space mission in an isolated self-sufficient environment. The following year saw a similar Sea Base project simulating life in an undersea research station.

Employers are increasingly concerned about the quality of high school graduates. According to the Public Agenda Report (1998), 68 percent of high school graduates are not prepared for the workforce, and 52 percent lack the basic skills for college. The National Assessment Governing Board reported in 1997 that 43 percent of all high school students scored below basic achievement levels. CEO America, the Children's Educational Opportunity Foundation, helps provide low-income parents with opportunity scholarships—giving them a choice as to where their children attend elementary and secondary schools. For more information, visit www.ceoamerica.org.[15]

When this kind of outreach can be linked to students who are children or siblings of current employees, the projects take on a whole new meaning. As employees become directly involved, they are also learning and growing with company support. See chapter nine to explore more opportunities for community outreach.

CLEAR THE WAY
FOR FAST TRACKERS

Many organizations are fortunate enough to have some bright shining stars in their workforce. These special people are the fast learners, the top producers, the potential future leaders of the organization. They deserve—and need—special treatment to keep them satisfied, challenged, and committed to their employers. As good as they are, recruiters from other companies will soon target them and try to entice them away.

Solution: provide them with as many growth opportunities as they want. Let them rise quickly in the organization, but be sure they have the education and training to support whatever work they move into. If you just let them run without strong support, sooner or later you'll be setting them up for failure. Even fast trackers can go only so long before hitting bumps in the road or quicksand. It's at that point that you can be at the greatest risk of losing them and your investment in their success and their future.

Assign at least one seasoned executive or manager to watch over these special people. This person will act not only as a mentor, but also as a controller, who helps the fast tracker grow without getting himself into trouble. The mentor's job is to encourage, teach, and shape, while preventing the protégé from getting into risky, deep water.

Beware of the feelings other employees may have for these people who will probably enjoy a certain level of favoritism and privileges. Collaboration will be important, but so will understanding. This fast growth could reveal some sensitive areas for other employees who feel they're being passed over unfairly. Human resource professionals should keep a watchful eye on all affected personnel.

Make Learning Convenient

Take steps to make learning as convenient as possible. This concept includes physical, time, and environmental convenience.

Physical convenience means holding classes in places that are easy to get to, with nearby safe parking, if parking is a consideration. Training rooms should be easy to find, clearly marked, and certainly fully accessible for disabled participants. Arrangements made with colleges or universities to bring classes into the workplace can make those courses more convenient for employees. If you have a lending library of books, tapes, and other learning materials, it should be easy to find and use.

> At the American Express Call Center in Greensboro, North Carolina, a learning space is conveniently located inside the front door of the building. Materials can be borrowed from the library collection and employees can use computers for learning at any time.

Time convenience means that workplace learning sessions are scheduled at times that make sense for participants. In some organizations, this timing means holding classes that fit in the calendar for shift workers around the clock. Providing snacks—coffee and donuts or cheese and crackers—to acknowledge that people might be a bit hungry at learning time is appreciated and makes participants feel welcome.

> Employees of IHS HelpDesk Service, New York, can access training programs on-line using a password. The company also makes software easily available to their analysts to keep skills sharp as they serve their customers on-site across the country.

Environmental convenience refers to the work environment and the culture. Supervisors and managers must support learning and facilitate an employee's missing work to attend classes. If the employee thinks that the training and development is a burden or an irritant to the supervisor, the employee may choose to keep the boss happy and forego the training.

Take-home training and self-study courses can address all of these issues. With a supervisor's encouragement, the worker takes learning materials home to use—at a time and place convenient to the worker. This kind of learning support can also be valuable to workers who are dispersed or who usually work at home or in a satellite workcenter.

Set Standards for Developing *All* Employees

All employees, not just managers or salespeople, should have growth opportunities available to them. In today's tight job market, employers cannot afford to treat any employees as commodities which can be turned over and replaced by other workers. Everyone must be valued, which means everyone must benefit from training and education in the workplace. As we said before, growth plans should be developed for each employee.

In those cases where there is a limited amount of knowledge and skill required for the job, learning opportunities could concentrate on future position possibilities and on personal development. Courses or seminars on listening, time management, organization skills, driving safety, and similar topics will be valuable for all employees.

Establish standards that confirm that all employees will have at least some learning opportunities each year. Having a learning environment means that everyone benefits and everyone grows.

Everyone Is a Teacher

Just as everyone is a learner, everyone is a teacher. Each of us has a lot to learn, but we also have knowledge, skills, and techniques we can share with others. Wherever possible, create conditions where employees can teach each other. Acknowledge their knowledge base and their intellectual and experiential value to the employer. Provide chances for workers to share what they know with others. Some employees won't take advantage of the opportunity, but others will.

It feels good to learn, and it feels good to help other people learn. On both sides of this coin, workers build their self-esteem, their sense of having value, of making a contribution to the employer they chose to join. Remember that employees are making choices every day about what company they'll join, how much they'll do, and how long they'll stay. Environments that foster collaborative learning encourage people to stay and to make a difference for each other, as well as for the employer.

Today's employee needs—no, requires—multiple and varied

opportunities for growth and learning in the workforce. Employers of Choice will recognize these needs and act accordingly, benefiting both workers and employers in the short and long run.

The Virginia suburbs of Washington, D. C., have become a high tech corridor. The need for trained people is insatiable; practically every information technology (IT) company in Northern Virginia has a serious need for workers. A 1998 study showed 22,987 vacancies in just over 2,000 firms. The Northern Virginia Regional Partnership, a coalition of educators and local technology executives, formed in 1997, was awarded a $2.4 million state grant for technological education and workforce development.

The objective is to attract and train new workers, particularly those in non-technical jobs who want to transition to careers in information technology. The vehicle is a 6-month crash course called Technology Retraining Internship Program (TRIP). Launched in January 1998, the program seeks to move students into work quickly through hands-on training in paid internships with local IT companies. These practical experiences supplement classroom learning so that students, who already have business experience in other fields, can become productive quickly. By July 1999, 90 students had graduated from the first four sessions and 81 were employed with local IT companies at salaries averaging $35,400.[16]

Collaborate with Colleges and Universities

Community colleges and state universities are usually in the mainstream when it comes to preparing people to perform in the local workforce. Workforce development efforts are even stronger now in the tight labor market environment.

These locally focused schools will develop courses of study around the needs of area employers. If there is a great need for a particular skill and the jobs are available, the educators respond. Most of the work is done by community colleges, so that would be a good place to start to talk with people.

If the courses are already available, you can send your employees as students. Often the sessions are held at times that are convenient for people who are already working. If you have enough employee-students, instructors can be sent to your facilities or special classes can be scheduled on campus for your company. See the reference to CIGNA-Penn program earlier in this chapter.

Another option is to send prospective employees to the classes before you hire them. You may want to award scholarships for them to take the training before hiring, so these new hires are ready to work when you put them on the payroll. If they are not successful in the training classes, your risk has been minimized.

People looking for a new career may take courses at a local institution, and then come to you for a job. Arrangements might be made through the college placement office. To gain experience and test a relationship with your company, these students may want to work as interns. These fixed-term assignments are usually good for interns, the college, and the employer. Our firm has employed interns almost every semester since the mid-1980s; we've gained from their work and we've enjoyed helping them grow.

> The Community College of Philadelphia responded to a need in the hospitality industry for training for desk clerks and other entry-level workers. Thousands of jobs have been created by the growth of the industry in the Philadelphia area; hospitality programs at Drexel, Temple, and Widener Universities as well as the University of Delaware have become more focused on the bachelor and master's degree levels.[17]

Notes

1. "The 90-day checkup," *Inc.* Magazine, March 1999, p. 111.
2. Jeanne C. Meister, "Ten Steps to Creating a Corporate University," *Training and Development* Magazine, November 1998.
3. Lisa Holton, "Keeping It Current: A Commitment to Continuous Training is Helping Companies Retain the Most Promising Workers in a Tight Labor Market," Chicago *Tribune*, November 5, 1998/
4. On the Mind column, Carol Pine, Saint Paul *Pioneer Press*, January 17, 1999.
5. *Ibid.*
6. "Corporate Universities—More and Better," *Workforce Magazine*, May 1998, p. 16.
7. Jodi Speigel Arthur, "Virtual U," *Human Resource Executive*, March 19, 1998, p. 44.
8. Survey Results: How is Coaching Used in Your Organization? Lee Hecht Harrison, 1999.
9. "Moving Up Through Mentoring," *Workforce* Magazine, March 1998, p. 36.
10. *Ibid*, p. 42.
11. "Brushing Up on the Three R's," *HR Magazine*, October 1999, p. 82.

12. *Ibid.*

13. Julie Cook, "Peer Influence," Human Resource Executive, May 18, 1999, p. 56.

14. Lynn Densford, "AT CIGNA, education is a much-valued benefit," *Corporate University Review*, May–June 1998.

15. CEO American, Post Office Box 1543, Bentonville, Arkansas 72712, (501) 273-6957.

16. "Novices Fill Technology Gaps," *HR Magazine*, November 1999, p. 74.

17. James M. O'Neill, "Colleges are answering hotel industry's SOS," *The Philadelphia Inquirer*, October 28, 1999, p. D1.

MEANINGFUL WORK

With all the choices about what kind of work they might perform, more and more people are looking for meaningful work. Meaningful work? In many organizations, that's a strange term—something new, different and confusing. For Employers of Choice, having meaningful work to do means that practically every task performed by every employee has value. That value may be serving a customer, maintaining machinery so everything runs smoothly, keeping records that support the company's financial health, or directly producing goods or providing services that make the world a better place, for somebody.

Meaningful work doesn't necessarily mean that the tasks performed by each individual are life-changing for some internal or external customer. It's a bigger picture, a larger sense, a deeper feeling of making a positive difference through your work. This feeling can be experienced by senior executives and janitors alike. In fact, janitors often feel their work has more impact—they can see the results—than the work done by "the suits" occupying those corner offices. The message here is that everyone can feel that their work is meaningful, regardless of the actual work they're doing or their position in the organization.

Meaningfulness is a personal thing. It is an attitude, a thought process, "If I can get the extraneous junk out of my way so I can concentrate on real work, I'll be a lot happier. I'll be happier staying with my employer if *I* can make a personal difference." To enable this opportunity, routine busywork is substantially reduced through the use of technology. Each worker is able to invest a higher proportion of his or her time in doing positive, exciting things that count. The following are ways to help give each worker in your organization opportunities for meaningful work.

Things that happen to us personally often make a difference in our business lives. In 1991, just after he got a promotion at Land O' Lakes, Dan Hanson learned that he had cancer. It was a wake-up call. "It gave me a sense of urgency. I knew that I had to rediscover the meaning of my work." He took six months off, beat the cancer, and rejuvenated his career. He returned to Land O' Lakes and began teaching business classes at a college. He also wrote two books that are on our recommended reading list in this book.

Hanson became president of the fluid-dairy division of Land O' Lakes and discovered a troubling problem: "People didn't seem to be finding meaning in work, they didn't seem to be shining, and there was an energy missing." Believing that the problem wasn't with the people, but with oppressive work environments, he concentrated on helping people feel more connected with their work. He highlighted "pockets of wellness" where teams changed how they did things. Then he focused on building communities from the ground up and genuinely recognizing people who were doing well. Hanson emphasizes, "One important thing I've learned is that people want to be challenged, as well as appreciated."[1]

PROVIDE OPPORTUNITIES TO MAKE A POSITIVE DIFFERENCE

Practically every organization is involved in some sort of work that makes a positive difference in the world. Sometimes the benefit to others is direct and obvious; sometimes the benefit is less tangible or helps another organization make a difference. Directly or indirectly, you can determine how each employee makes a difference.

Armed with the knowledge of what your people do to make a difference, talk personally with each employee about his or her contribution. Validate the importance of that contribution. Help them comprehend how significant they are to the achievement of meaningful results for the company as a whole.

Wherever possible, provide feedback for employees about how they made a difference, how they had an influence, an impact, on the end result of the organization's work. Help people see what *they* did and how *their* accomplishments contributed to the end result.

For those employees not directly involved in making a difference through their work, create opportunities for them to be involved in some influential work of the company. Perhaps they could spend some time—on partial assignment or a temporary special assignment—working directly with those who are beneficiaries of the company's work. Or perhaps they can be recruited for a company-sponsored public service project such as cleaning a roadside, building picnic tables for a local park, or helping to build a house with Habitat for Humanity.

Concentrate on Measurable Results

Find ways to measure the work performed by every employee. Determine how you can measure the results or the impact of the work so people can measure their own performance, their own impact on the world around them. When people can see the results of their work, that they've accomplished something, they feel more valuable and productive.

A powerful linkage with this results-measuring approach is the practice of goal setting. This process starts at the top of the organization with strategic visioning and corporate goal-setting, but can flow very effectively throughout the entire company. When people set goals and objectives, and design a process to achieve those aims, they gain a stronger sense of purpose. As those targets are reached, workers feel satisfied.

Employers of Choice seek to satisfy employees in many ways. Seeing the results of their work builds an intrinsic satisfaction, enabling employees to have a sense of accomplishment.

> In the 1980s, at the Volvo Heavy Truck manufacturing plants in Orrville, Ohio, the general manager was William P. "Phil" Mayes . Realizing that his stamping plant employees didn't really appreciate the end result of their work, Phil brought a finished Class 8 semi-tractor into the stamping plant. Each employee was able to see how the part he was working on fit on the truck. They developed a sense of pride, as if their name was on each piece. Phil used the fresh-off-the-assembly-line truck to take randomly-selected employees to lunch at a local restaurant each month. Workers got to ride in a truck they helped build.

Provide Intellectual Challenges

For years, many workers perceived an imaginary sign at the entrance to their workplace admonishing people to check their brains at the door. The impression was that employers didn't want people to think, just to perform their duties as prescribed. Workers put up with this attitude, believing that mindless adherence to the rules, regulations, and procedures was the way to behave on the job.

This blind obedience may have been appropriate for some workers for a while, but it certainly isn't appropriate today. Today's jobs are more demanding, calling for people to think, make decisions, and exercise more control over their work and results. Most workers deliberately avoid the no-thinking jobs, preferring to engage in work that is mentally challenging. Even hourly laborers want to think about the best way to get a job done.

Wherever possible, challenge people to think. Encourage them to discover new ideas and new ways of doing tasks. Solicit ideas for improvement in all areas, acknowledge them, and implement the ideas wherever appropriate, as soon as possible. Instead of telling workers each step of project completion or job accomplishment, let them figure it out for themselves. Thinking, then acting and achieving results energizes workers, building their competence, confidence, and commitment. Those powerful feelings lead to employment longevity and higher performance that makes the company a better place for everyone.

America's electrical utilities are being deregulated, substantially changing the culture of the organizations. No longer can utility companies take customers for granted, assuming that they'll always be there, captive. Now the utilities will shift to a competitive mode, a major difference in the way they do business—and an intellectual transformation must take place. Niagara Mohawk, a gas and electric utility in Syracuse, New York, initiated a process to change the way employees think. They placed articles from the *Wall Street Journal* in employee newsletters on a regular basis and arranged for the company's senior executives to discuss deregulation topics with groups of employees.

The company's human resource staff, under the direction of senior vice president David J. Arrington, designed a day-long seminar titled "Understanding Power Choice." The seminar, mandatory for all 8,600 of the utility's employees, explores how each area of the company makes money under the present system, and how those areas expect to make money under deregulation. All employees also attended a crash course in basic finance and accounting to give them a better grasp of business fundamentals.[2]

Encourage Collaboration

No one has all the answers. Working solo isn't always as much fun or even as effective as working with one or more colleagues to complete tasks. When things are moving very quickly, it's reassuring to have input from others, to share what's being developed and accomplished.

People like to invite co-workers to join in projects, to help get certain things done that they can't do themselves (or can't do as well themselves). They will naturally form teams to accomplish results. Most workers prefer to create their own teams, rather than have team composition determined by an outside force such as a manager or executive.

There are a few things you can do to encourage collaboration, beyond spreading the word that collaboration is a good thing. Sometimes a few physical supports will make it easier for people to collaborate.

Provide informal meeting places where collaborators can sit and talk. This venue could be a traditional meeting room with a table and chairs, or it could be a grouping of stuffed chairs, sofas, and throw pillows forming a conversation pit. Some organizations are enlarging the sizes of cubicle offices to create room for visitors to gather and brainstorm ideas, solve problems, or simply discuss their work with each other. If your facilities are in a campus-like setting or if you have a park nearby, outdoor environments are often conducive to high levels of comfortable communication and interaction between people.

Support collaboration by establishing communications systems for sharing ideas and information. The mechanics of such a system can range from a bulletin board to sophisticated software applications across a local area network (LAN) or wide area network (WAN) linking your company's computers.

Clarify Expectations

When people have a clear understanding of what's expected of them, and when they have the support they need from co-workers and superiors, they usually do an outstanding job. Look closely at the most successful companies you know and you'll discover that people see the big picture, they know what's expected of them and they have an agreement about what they can expect from others. The results are tremendous!

Each employee should be familiar with the organization's overall mission and plan. They'll be better team members if they can see that they are playing an important role, that they're an integral part of the overall system.

An effective way to help employees comprehend the big picture is to give them an all-encompassing tour of your company. Explain how the company gets business, how the orders come in, and how they're processed for invoicing and manufacturing (or service). Tell them about the purchasing function and show them how materials are brought in at the receiving area. After they get a look at how materials move into processing or are moved into another area for stocking, show employees each step of the process. Show them all the important areas of the company, including accounting, customer service, maintenance, and the president's office. Define what happens in each place so learners can put the pieces together in their minds. Message: it's valuable to help blue collar workers appreciate that white collar and pink collar workers do real work, and vice-versa.

Obviously, the elements of what you do will be different for each company. Help people understand how the whole system works, then show them what their roles are. This approach enables each worker to appreciate the value and importance of the work they do—as it interconnects with everything else the company does. This knowledge substantially reduces the "it's just another job" attitude, and raises self-esteem as people recognize that others are depending on them to do their part. Absenteeism drops when workers know others are relying on them so the whole company can function.

When people see that big picture, it's also easier for them to suggest improvements in the way your company does business. Educated in what you're trying to accomplish in your business, employees can offer valuable suggestions for doing things better, differently, or for different reasons. They'll have a better view of company functions, and they'll be thinking and planning toward future success.

Hold People Accountable

Employers of Choice are characterized by high levels of accountability—at all levels. It's not just for those in management; accountability is for everyone. The lower you push accountability in your organization, the more effective and involved your people will be.

Seek ways to heighten feelings of personal accountability for every employee. Help everyone understand what is expected, and when, and that you hold each person accountable for fulfilling his or her part of the task. When each person meets those expectations, those accountabilities, three things will happen.

> As profiled in chapter five, the Nordstrom Company, headquartered in Seattle, Washington, pushes accountability down to the lowest level, their front-line salespeople. These empowered employees are given the authority to do *whatever it takes* to satisfy their discriminating customers. There are stories of Nordstrom people accepting returns on merchandise they never sold in order to placate a customer.

1. Each employee will have a sense of making a personal, significant contribution to the group effort, a real sense of pride and satisfaction;
2. You, as a leader, will be developing your people and accomplishing the objectives expected of your team by *your* leader; and
3. The organization will fulfill its goals as a consequence of everyone working together as a team to accomplish the job.

Vigorously fight the tendency to have "upward-climbing monkeys" in your organization. These monkeys are the tasks and decisions—the accountabilities—that many people attempt to pass on to others, especially their superiors. Keep that accountability down where it belongs by training supervisors, managers, and executives to insist that their people figure things out for themselves, with help as needed. Help people learn how to do things on their own and they'll become less dependent and more accountable.

One way to encourage accountability is to have people—at all levels—report on what they've accomplished and how they've performed in comparison to their goals and objectives. By making these public expressions part of the organizational culture, you emphasize accountability and recognize that people choose to be accountable as members of your organization.

STRETCH PEOPLE TO REACH THEIR FULL POTENTIAL

Most people do not work to their fullest potential. While some of the reason results from personal motivation, quite a bit can be attributed to organizational culture and leadership. Change that level of performance, the accepted standard, and you've made a positive difference. When people are continually stimulated and inspired to do their best, they and their employers will be substantially more successful as a consequence.

People feel great about stretching to be all they can be, and this can be wonderful as long as that extra effort is congruent with the culture of their employer. Be demanding in a firm and positive way. Set workers' sights high and assist them in achieving tasks they might have thought were beyond their capabilities. Be enthusiastic with your support, emphasizing shared responsibilities and personal accountability to self, co-workers, leaders, and the organization as a whole.

Create a feeling of personal achievement, support and focus on team goals, and people will gradually begin to assume more and more initiative. It probably won't happen by itself; you will have to clear the path so people feel comfortable doing things on their own. Celebrate high achievement on a personal and team basis to bring high achievement and high potential-realization into the open.

Stimulate Creativity

There's lots of talk about creativity, but does it really work as well as we're led to believe? Inspiring creative thinking and subsequent performance has several significant benefits for Employers of Choice. First, companies that encourage creativity attract a higher caliber of employee—the people who want to work in that kind of an exciting environment. Second, people who thrive in an innovative atmosphere want to stay in their jobs, continually exploring new and better ways to do things. And third, creative people—individually, and even more powerfully together—drive higher efficiency, new products and services, corporate reputations, and bottom line results.

We like the characterization of the turtle in explaining creativity. In our consulting work, we use the turtle as a sort of icon to remind people to stick their necks out. Turtles don't make progress until they stick their necks out. They're protected by their hard shells; it's okay to take risks. This concept can be a positive, energizing expression.

Management must be willing and supportive in its message to encourage risk-taking. Action must follow words. If you encourage innovation, then discipline people for taking a chance on a new process or approach, you'll dampen enthusiasm and results. This endorsement of creativity and risk-taking must be real in an Employer of Choice organization. If the support is not genuine, people will see right through the phoniness and will leave—psychologically and physically.

If you're serious about stimulating creativity, consider using the turtle image. Get some posters of turtles, stuffed turtles, plastic or ceramic turtles. Put them in your office and display them in other areas of your facilities. Send them to people in the field. Use turtle images in awards.

Remember that a key to inspiring creativity and initiative among your people is to be receptive to their new ideas. Nourish their thinking and bolster their performance in whatever ways seem appropriate. Your goal is to send a clear message that you respect the insight and mental capacity of your people and want to see those strengths used to improve working conditions and productivity.

Rotate Job Assignments

There's a restlessness in today's workforce, a desire to move around from job to job more frequently than we've seen in the past. Respond to that desire by giving employees opportunities to change jobs *within* your organization. Enable them to manage their own career development by trying new jobs at *their* discretion. Give them a safety net to fall back to their earlier work if the new assignment doesn't work out for some reason.

You can take this concept even further and *require* job rotation. This approach is particularly effective in work groups where people perform different jobs that fit together to produce an end result. Arrange for workers to exchange jobs periodically so they can understand and appreciate what other workers do. As they build proficiency in other roles, these workers can become more cohesive and productive as a team. The strength of the team will act as a glue to hold them together as a stable unit, reducing potential employee turnover. Because of their enriched experience, these valuable workers will choose to stay.

We've heard of companies that cross-train almost all their employees and change roles even during the day. One manufacturer produces its product in daily batches. Everyone pitches in to get the process started early in the morning, shifting to different tasks as the day—and the batch—progress. By the end of the day, the same team operates in the role of the shipping department, preparing their product for movement to the customer. When fewer people are needed during particular parts of the process, the extra people help out in accounting, maintenance, or other tasks that need to be done in the company. Everyone enjoys variety, teamwork, and results every day, and the workers choose to remain with their employer.

Empower High Performers

Employers of Choice quite naturally want to attract and hold people who could be described as "employees of choice." With the demand for top talent, it's important to give more to these more valued workers. We're not talking about more money; we're talking about more power. With more authority to get things done, these high performers can experience greater accomplishment—benefiting themselves and their employer.

"Empowerment," the buzzword of the 1990s, is an appropriate word to describe the concept that will attract, optimize, and retain the most desirable workers. The idea here is to give people access to information, the availability of the resources they need, and the capacity to make the decisions necessary to get things done. People with high potential want to keep moving in their work. They have little patience for waiting for approval from senior people on small decisions that they feel should be within their power.

Examine your approval requirements. Are there some changes you can make to streamline the process, to get more power in the hands of those closer to the problems being solved? We've found client organizations with as many as seventeen approval levels—seventeen different people had to sign-off on decisions before projects could move to the next step! If you're an aggressive high performer, you don't have the patience to wait for seventeen busy people to find time to approve and pass the paperwork along to the next person.

Hint: Invite people at the lower levels of the approval chain to offer suggestions for improvement. They can probably identify the bottlenecks and recommend more efficient methods to direct power and speed to those who need the support.

SUPPORT DECENTRALIZED POWER

Decentralization is to organizations what empowerment is to individuals. The centralization-decentralization argument has been around for years, and will continue to be a topic in management meetings for years to come. The current trend is toward creating autonomous units within larger organizations, that is, decentralization.

An advantage of decentralization for the Employer of Choice is the opportunity to build a network of smaller, more cohesive, business units. In these less-populated organizations, workers can become closer, more interdependent, and more linked to achievable goals and objectives. A greater sense of community develops, as does a stronger dedication to working together to get the job done. The enthusiasm that characterizes these smaller organizations is similar to the drive felt in entrepreneurial firms. It can be very positive, motivational, and attractive for present and future employees.

A potential disadvantage of decentralization is that workers don't feel as connected to the larger organization. This risk can be overcome through corporate identification programs, good communication with other business units and with the corporate entity, and periodic visits from corporate officials. Corporate identification can include positioning such as "Smaller Organization, a proud unit of Larger Organization." Logo clothing and similar identification products can be offered, including the name of the larger company and perhaps the name of the decentralized unit as well.

> Pursuing a higher level of strategic agility, Noble & Associates previously mentioned in chapter five, reorganized. The reorganization into quality teams was instrumental to their current success. Smaller business units enable the company to be faster and more responsive to client needs.

While it's fine to decentralize power, it's important to note the strength of close association with the parent organization. It may be necessary to discuss these issues with people at both organizations to help them understand the power and value of symbiosis. There are benefits to both the parent and the decentralized units for them to remain associated and supportive. It's important that all concerned understand the big picture of the relationship.

OFFER STIMULATING OPPORTUNITIES

Challenge people. Stimulate them with assignments that are out of the ordinary. Give them opportunities to break new ground, to design and test new processes, to create new products or services, and to organize things in different ways.

Individual special assignments can be stimulating, but team assignments can offer even more excitement. When giving the team the "charge," describe the opportunity or the desired results. Then let the members of the group design their own approach.

It's not necessary to actually give specific assignments. In discussions with members of management, explore how you might create a stimulating environment in which to work. Your leadership team can create a stimulating place to be by attitude, expectation, and the way management responds as people perform. Encourage people to think and to solve problems.

Stimulate thinking by inviting employees from a number of departments to join in problem-solving or brainstorming sessions. Praise their intellectual performance, then reinforce your support by sharing team output with others. You might even invite more comment, further enhancing the stimulating environment of the organization.

FOCUS ON THE CUSTOMER

The whole concept of focusing on the customer is common knowledge in every organization. Of course, the sense of the vital importance of the customer is also central to every Employer of Choice. The intense concentration on customer delight is expected by the kind of workers desired by preferred employers. It's a mutually satisfying perspective.

Two points are worth noting as we talk about customer focus. First, don't take for granted that everyone "gets the customer thing." Use internal marketing techniques to emphasize the value and show employees in every position how to bring the concept to life. Engage everyone in delivering outstanding service to customers.

The other point is that your company has *internal* as well as *external* customers. Not everyone in the organization comes in contact with the external customers—the outside people or companies that purchase the company's goods and services. Everyone does, however, have contact with the internal customers—fellow employees. Building a strong customer service attitude internally will foster greater cooperation between departments, among employees. Everyone will feel more welcome and supported, engendering a corporate culture that people don't want to abandon by working somewhere else.

FOCUS ON RESULTS

A conscious aspect of meaningful work is the opportunity to produce results that are meaningful. An organization-wide focus on the results you're trying to achieve will convey a stronger sense of purpose, of meaning, into the work being done.

Results are usually measurable, providing the opportunity to track progress and evaluate achievements. Share information about accomplishments, and comparison to goals, with all employees. As they have more knowledge and gain more understanding about what everyone's trying to do and how they're doing, people tend to be more committed to achieving the shared objectives.

When a company focuses more on activity than on results, workers concentrate on process instead of the finished product. It's easy to get bogged down in detail and quickly lose any sense of accomplishment. Work piles up, there's no end in sight, and motivation drops dramatically. Under these conditions, seeing no value to the mountains of work they're doing, employees will choose to leave the organization. With today's freedom of movement, it's not difficult for competent people to find new jobs easily and quickly.

Interview employees to discover what results they see in their work. Whenever you find someone who doesn't realize meaningful results from his or her efforts, make whatever changes are necessary so that all workers see a personal contribution flowing from their investment of time, expertise, and energy.

EXPAND AND ENRICH JOBS

The workers of today and tomorrow don't want to be limited. They don't want to be forced to stay in little cubbyholes that define who they are, and by definition, who they cannot be.

This shift, which will be seen in organizations recognized as Employers of Choice, is to move from job descriptions to *role* descriptions that are much broader in scope. Roles will be more focused on results to be accomplished, accountabilities and a relationship with the overall objectives of the company. There may be an emphasis on specialization, but role descriptions will encourage workers to cross whatever imaginary lines they find in organizations to accomplish the mission.

We'll see leadership roles, supporting roles, coordinative roles, design roles, sales and marketing roles, production roles, logistics and material handling roles, training roles, administrative roles, and more. Limitations will be lifted, providing the freedom to construct whatever kind of work relationship makes sense at the time.

One of the components of role descriptions might be a set of competencies to be mastered. This sort of structure facilitates a training and development intention: the mastery of competencies enables employees to move to higher levels and the opportunity to do more complicated or different types of jobs. The ability to engage in many different kinds of tasks is meaningful for workers who don't want to be type-cast, limited, or tied down to any particular job, occupation, or career path. They will have choices, as appreciated by people working for Employers of Choice.

Eliminate Restrictive Policies and Procedures

People working for Employers of Choice are pleased that policies and procedures are supportive and rarely obstruct progress or the achievement of measurable results. So-called red tape bogs down organizational operations and decision making, confusing and frustrating those who are struggling valiantly to get things accomplished.

People working in organizations that are bound in red tape reach a point where they just give up. They're so turned off by the organization's perceived lack of responsiveness and inability to get things done that they lose their own motivation to try to make things better. They may still collect their paychecks, but only their bodies are present at work; their souls, their hearts, are simply not in the race anymore. They're just putting in their time.

With today's labor shortage, the more competent and self-initiated workers are leaving red-tape organizations. Think about who will remain if all the self-starters leave. Imagine trying to run a bureaucratically-hampered organization with a workforce comprised of marginally competent workers! Incredible as it may sound, there are still a lot of companies, government agencies, and not-for-profit organizations that still operate that way!

To attack this problem in your organization, you might start with a survey, then move to focus groups. Ask people what gets in their way of becoming high performers. Listen carefully, take notes, and watch for similarities in responses. The focus groups can bring out the relationship between various barriers to achievement. In some cases, the obstacles will be methods installed in hopes of eliminating the very problems they accentuated.

As you learn where the red tape is, eliminate it. Find out what's getting in the way and get it out of the way—now! As employees see that you are sincere, they'll open up with more and more problems to be resolved. Gradually, you'll clean up your system and work can proceed efficiently. As you remove the congestion, everything will flow more smoothly and you'll enjoy the progress that attracts and holds the employees you want.

Don't simply try to work around blockages. Remove them. Remember, red tape is not biodegradable. It will continue to obstruct your systems unless you eliminate it.

Establish Tight Links Among Work, Mission, Goals, and Profits

People who work for an Employer of Choice understand clearly how their personal work makes a difference for the organization. They understand the company mission and the vision that propels the organization into the future. These employees enjoy an appreciation and respect for what the employer is all about and where it's going. In most cases, they've participated in the design of the future direction and therefore, support it fully and enthusiastically.

When workers understand their goals and objectives, they can better manage their daily work, with the comforting and energizing knowledge that what they do each day contributes to their expected overall accomplishment and the company's goals. Knowing that your effort fits with what everyone else is doing substantially adds to the meaningfulness of what you do. The powerful sense of congruence makes it all worthwhile.

Alignment of all the various functions of an organization with the mission, vision, and goals strengthens performance and accomplishment. Senior executives continually strive to achieve this alignment, but that's not enough. To make this concept really work, the linkage has to be felt, experienced, and supported right down to the front-line hourly worker.

If the organization is a profit-making company, the focus should, of course, be on generating the profits targeted by senior management. Each employee should appreciate how his or her work helps the company reach profit goals. Where appropriate, compensation can be based, in part, on contribution to profit achievement.

THANK PEOPLE FOR MAKING A DIFFERENCE

The kinds of people recruited to work for an Employer of Choice are often self-starters. They look for the best opportunities and expect to work smart—and hard—to get things done. They're already self-motivated and enjoy intrinsic rewards of personal accomplishment.

Still, these high performers want to be appreciated by their employer. To retain them, and motivate them, thank them for being part of your team. Thank them for the specific work they do. Thank them for making a difference. Honor and respect them as valuable members of the organization.

Acknowledge the special people you want to keep by giving them the tools to get their jobs done with effi-

Sometimes the mission isn't about profits at all. An increasing number of companies and their people are working for deeper reasons. More than 40 years ago, a purpose-driven leader named Earl Bakken formed a company called Medtronic, a manufacturer of medical products. The mission statement he wrote in 1960, which has not been changed since, declares that the company's purpose is to "restore people to the fullness of life and health." Even though he's retired, Bakken still meets with every new employee worldwide and leads three-hour sessions with groups of 15 to 20 employees where he describes the founding purpose of the company.

"The most meaningful event of the year for Medtronic's employees is the annual holiday party where employees hear the personal stories of the patients whose lives have been saved and restored by Medtronic products. Bill George, president and CEO, stresses 'leading by values' rather than 'management by objectives.' Medtronic values (in order) are 'restoring people to full health, serving your customers with products and services of unsurpassed quality, recognizing the personal worth of employees, making a fair profit and return for shareholders, and maintaining good citizenship as a company.'"[3]

ciency, effectiveness, and a high degree of satisfaction. Empower them, support them, create and maintain the culture that will make what they do so much fun that they look forward to going to work every day.

The ultimate in demonstrating appreciation for employees came when Malden Mills Industries, Lawrence, Massachusetts, suffered a $300 million fire that destroyed its manufacturing plant. Suddenly, thousands of families and thousands of employees were impacted directly and indirectly. In a move that is now legendary, Malden owner Aaron Fuerstein promised to keep all employees on the payroll and rebuild the plant, which makes Polartec fabric. The following year, Malden opened a new $100 million plant on the site of the old building. All but a few of the 1,400 employees returned.[4]

Notes

1. *Fast Company* Magazine, December 1998, p. 192.
2. "Re-charged and Ready," *Human Resource Executive* Magazine, May 19, 1998, p. 24.
3. Rhonda K. Miller, "Workers to Be Paid While Comapny Rebuilds," *At Work*, October 1993, p. 13.
4. *Human Resource Executive* Magazine, April 1999.

COMPENSATION AND BENEFITS

Compensation and benefits have always been considered a vital part of the relationship between employer and employee. The emphasis in Employer of Choice organizations is on fairness, competitiveness, comprehensiveness, and uniqueness.

A poll taken by the Gallup organization for *Inc.* Magazine reported that 74 percent of American workers think they're fairly paid. Only slightly more men—76 percent, than women—71 percent, said they were compensated fairly last year. This result is somewhat surprising when you consider reports that women continue to lag behind men in average wages, earning 74 cents to each man's dollar.[1]

Every worker is concerned about what compensation will be earned when working for an employer. It's a natural issue when considering the exchange of value between a worker and an employer. The worker brings certain education, expertise, experience, energy, and capacity to the relationship with the employer. Based on a variety of conditions, the worker's package has a value to the employer. That value is expressed in the compensation package provided by the employer to the worker. It's not just a standard hours-for-pay

An April 1999 survey of senior human resource executives attending the American Management Association's (AMA) annual Human Resources Conference revealed some interesting information. Retention was a "very serious" issue in 46 percent of the companies represented at the conference, and a "serious" issue in another 28 percent. Looking historically, 64 percent of the respondents said retention was a greater concern than a year before, and 65 percent expected retention to gain in importance over the coming year.

Survey results showed that companies with employee retention programs say they find educational and lifestyle incentives more effective than dollars and cents compensation. Technical training, employability training, and flexible work arrangements were perceived as most effective, significantly ahead of stock incentives and even pay for performance programs.

"Investing in employees' futures is more important than immediate compensation," said Eric Rolfe Greenberg, AMA's Director of Management Studies. "Programs that improve work skills and future career development are seen as particularly effective."[2]

consideration anymore; there's a lot more to a comprehensive compensation arrangement in an Employer of Choice environment.

THE COMPENSATION PACKAGE

Pay (cash in the pocket) is certainly a significant part of the compensation package. Employers of Choice, though, recognizing the broader range of employee needs and interests, offer much more than just a high dollar wage or salary. There are many other components of the compensation package that have an equal or—for some people—higher value than the money.

Each employee's package is negotiated individually and, to an extent, independently. While there are standard guidelines, they're used in a more general way rather than serving as strict guidelines. Included in the package are the traditional pay and health insurance benefits, but quite a bit more is mixed in as employers become more creative, competitive, and sensitive to what workers want and need.

In some organizations, you might even get the sense that there's a return to the paternalistic orientation that characterized so many entrepreneurial companies in the middle and later years of the twentieth century. The owner regarded his employees almost as his own children; he loaned them money, visited with their families, and was concerned about their every need. Employers of Choice build a sense of community that is not dissimilar to the paternalistic model.

Competitive Pay

We tend to base much of our value as workers on how much money we're paid for doing our job. The dollar amounts have been a benchmark for comparison for generations. And we do compare our income to what we've earned on other jobs and what others are earning.

Some workers place an inordinate amount of value on the dollar amount they earn, since it's the only measure they have of their worth as an employee. This tendency is particularly prevalent in environments where supervisors don't do the human relations things—like saying "thank you"—to acknowledge workers' contributions. When you have no other sense of appreciation, of compensation, you tend to place more emphasis on the measure that is used—cash.

Other employers, seeking to recruit your employees, will quite naturally begin with large dollar offers. This bait sounds enticing, especially if the rest of the compensation package has not been valued and promoted. It's important to help your employees comprehend the "big picture" of the value they get working for you.

Nevertheless, pay must still be competitive. The first consideration must be to pay people what they're worth in the marketplace. A significant proportion of this pay will be in cash, though this doesn't mean you have to match or exceed other dollar offers. People have a sense for what they're worth, particularly if they've been checking around and interviewing. This figure will become a part of the negotiation process, but doesn't necessarily have to be paid in cash. Remember your total package and don't get hung up on pushing the dollars. Many great employees will happily take less cash in return for the non-cash compensation.

Pay must be comparative to the income levels in the community in which the employer is located. Much of the competitiveness concern will relate to the standard of living the employee can maintain in the community. Again, comparative comfort and positioning issues arise. The trend will be for people to live less extravagantly and more modestly, while investing more in savings programs, personal growth, and family activities. This shift is under way, but we'll go through a transition period before we see a strong movement toward lifestyle downsizing.

Conduct some research to learn about competitive pay rates in your area. Governmental agencies, chambers of commerce, trade groups, and others conduct these studies on a regular basis. Gather the information that relates to your company, then use it as a guide for what's reasonable. Determine what your strategy will be: will pay be at the top of the scale, better than average, or mid-range? Your initial pay and your overall strategy may influence your success in recruiting.

Performance-Based Pay

Paying for performance is not a new concept. Sales professionals have been paid on commission for many years. Now this compensation arrangement is being extended to positions outside the sales arena.

Employers are placing increasing emphasis on measurable performance. The philosophy is that everything is measurable in some way, from the work done by the CEO to the work done by the security guard, truck driver, secretary, or stock clerk. Given this approach, we can measure every job in some way to evaluate progress and achievement. With accurate, objective information, we can base part of every employee's compensation on personal achievement.

If performance can be fairly and objectively measured, then bonuses can be paid for various levels of achievement. Standards can be set for each job, establishing a minimal accepted level of performance. The employee must achieve that standard, or the employee's supervisor must take corrective action. Measurement levels can be set for various percentages of achievement above standard, with bonus compensation based on the measured level of performance during particular time periods.

For example, several workers may perform the same job. One of them operates at minimal standard and receives the base pay established for the position. Another functions at a measured level of 20 percent above the standard and receives a predetermined bonus assigned for that level of performance. A third employee is wonderfully proficient, performing at 55 percent above standard and enjoys a substantially higher bonus based on the measured achievement. All three are performing the work of the position, and they're being individually compensated based on their level of achievement. They're being paid for their performance.

The challenge with this concept is defining measurable objectives that can be used to fairly and accurately assess performance. Some positions, by their very nature, seem to defy measurement. Metrically-oriented human resource professionals assert that every position can be measured in some way.

Pay for Results

Another approach is to award bonuses for achieving specified quotas or objectives. In this scenario, management—preferably with the workers themselves involved—sets goals to be achieved. A wide range of goals can be set, from reducing costs to the number of customers served or calls handled, from a low number of complaints to increased sales. Whatever goals are most appropriate for the situation, they establish an agreed-upon target to be reached.

If the objective or quota is reached, a certain level of bonus is awarded to the employee(s) responsible for the achievement. If the target is surpassed, reached earlier, at higher quality, or some other measurement of improved performance, the bonus is enhanced by a pre-established amount. Goals and rewards must be set before the performance, if a pay-for-performance model is to be applied.

Bonuses may be given outside these parameters, but they'll be more subjective than objective. While these rewards may still be pay-for-performance or even pay-for-effort, the distinguishing factor of pay-for-performance compensation is the focus on pre-determined measurement and reward.

Profit-Related Accomplishment

Rather than pay out a lot of extra money or benefits for effort or job measurement, you might consider concentrating your offer of bonuses and incentives for *profit-related* accomplishment. The higher compensation goes to workers who are, directly or indirectly, enhancing the organization's profit. In profit-making companies, strengthening the bottom line is a critical reason for being in business.

Wherever possible, link rewards to achievement of profit. Connect what each employee does to profit generation. The more people understand the importance of a strong profit, and their personal influence on the company's profit, the more powerful will be the connection between personal performance and corporate success.

Some companies may find it valuable to pay company-wide bonuses based on corporate performance. Even if small amounts are paid to each employee, the message is clear: everyone contributes to company achievement. People choose to stay with employers where they feel their work makes a difference. With this kind of a connection between personal performance and corporate success, people can see how they make a difference.

Stock Options

When it comes to rewarding their workers, U.S. employers are now offering stock options to a wider number of employees, according to a survey from PricewaterhouseCoopers. Approximately 35 percent of the nearly 400 U.S.-based companies surveyed reported that they provide stock options to their non-exempt employees and also offer similar option plans for employees working outside of the United States. The intense competition for qualified workers is evident in the growing number of companies that include non-compete provisions in their stock options plans, which force employees to forfeit any stock options should they leave. According to the researchers, 74 of the surveyed companies had non-compete provisions. Among those companies, 54 extended the provisions to all participants in the option plan and not just to top-level executives.[3]

Profit-Sharing

Profit sharing is an increasingly popular way for employers to say thank you to employees for effective performance. It's an opportunity for employees to realize more of the fruits of their labors. There are a number of different distribution methods, perhaps the most popular being the 401(k) plans. Other alternatives are simple profit-sharing retirement plans without provisions for employee contributions and, of course, cash distributions on an annual or even more frequent basis. For small companies, the simpler plan is often a better way to go, particularly there are fewer than 25 employees and/or less than a million dollars in assets.

For small companies like Edelman's, a simple plan makes more sense than a 401(k). It can be set up for less than $2,000. A note of caution: once you get started, employees come to expect the benefit every year. A solution: link this benefit with the concept of open-book management so employees know exactly what the situation is, and how they might help change it, if necessary.

> The Edelman Group, an eight-employee marketing communications firm in New York, has a profit-sharing plan that makes employee turnover practically nonexistent among the firm's key people. Terri Edelman, owner, uses a simple plan that is funded entirely by the company. Each year she reviews the firm's finances with her accountant and determines what the contribution will be. During the past ten years, the company has had sales of about $2 million and distributed $500,000.[4]

Domestic Partner Benefits

Over the past few years, more and more employers have begun to offer domestic partner benefits. After meeting certain qualifications, particularly oriented toward confirming interdependence, partners of the same or different sex are covered by the company's benefit programs. Notable in this pioneering effort have been Digital, Disney, Bank of America, and the San Francisco 49ers. The time is right: the number of unmarried-couple households jumped from 1.6 million in 1980 to 4.2 million in 1998, according the U.S. Census Bureau, with one-third of those being same-sex partnerships. Only 9 percent of nongovernment employers nationwide offer this benefit.

> GTECH Holdings Corporation announced that it would extend health-care benefits to the domestic partners of its U.S. employees to promote diversity in the workplace. The largest lottery company in the world, the West Greenwich, Rhode Island, company employs 3,500 people in the United States. "We think it's another way for us to position ourselves as an Employer of Choice and an innovator," said spokesman Robert Rendine.[5]

OFFER DIRECT DEPOSITS OF PAYCHECKS

Running to the bank every payday can be a nuisance, especially in today's busy world. Direct deposit of checks is seen as an important bonus by a lot of workers today. We are aware of workers who when deciding between two equal jobs, chose the employer with direct deposit. She reasoned it was like receiving the gift of a couple of hours of time per month. Direct deposit streamlines the work of the accounting department and saves workers another bothersome errand. The issue here is convenience.

HELP EMPLOYEES ARRANGE FOR ELECTRONIC BILL PAYMENT

Some employees (not all) would be happy to pay more of their bills electronically. These services are provided by banks directly for their depositors. Getting to the bank to learn about such services and to make arrangements is another one of those time-consuming options on the I'll-get-to-it someday list. Bring the banks to your employees to make things easier for everyone. Invite each bank in your community to send representatives to your company's facilities on Banking Convenience Day, which can be whatever day you choose.

Promote the opportunity ahead of time, inviting your employees to schedule appointments with the representative of their bank. Appointment scheduling can be handled by human resources, by a receptionist with a sign-up sheet, or through a company intranet. This service will be entirely optional, with no obligations whatsoever on the part of the employee. Emphasize with the bankers that there is to be no high pressure selling; this is a service opportunity.

The company accounting department is not involved in these transactions. Arrangements are strictly confidential between the employee and the employee's bank. The company is merely making it more convenient for employees to meet with their bankers.

DIVERSIFY INSURANCE BENEFITS

Ensure that insurance offerings to prospective employees are varied and valuable. Benefits available could include options that follow.

Hospitalization and Major Medical

This benefit has become practically universal in employment compensation packages. There are many ways to provide medical coverage today, including traditional insurance, PPO, HMO, and other managed care plans.

In addition to the variety of options available, employers can also vary the degree of corporate participation in the premium cost. Some companies pay 100 percent of the costs, and some even fund uninsured medical expenses. Others pay for the employee's insurance, but ask the employee to pay for his or her dependents. In other situations, the proportion of the premium paid by the company increases with the employee's tenure. There are many ways to configure how this benefit is provided.

Life

Most comprehensive hospitalization and major medical plans include a life insurance benefit with the package. Beyond this level, employers can provide life insurance as a group benefit—company paid or payroll deduction, as split dollar key man policies where part of the benefit goes to the company and part goes to the employee's beneficiaries, or as individual policies paid by the company as part of the negotiated benefit package.

Dental

Most hospitalization plans do not include dental coverage. Going to the dentist is not a favorite activity for most of us, but we all know that we do have to take care of our teeth and gums. A regular schedule of checkups and cleanings, supplemented with whatever work has to be done on those nasty cavities, is one of those nagging necessities of life. With dental insurance coverage, there is a greater chance we'll take care of our precious teeth—and preserve all those beautiful smiles.

Dental insurance coverage may not be as expensive as you

think. It's available in the health insurance package from many companies, or from specialized providers such as Delta Dental Insurance Company.

Pet Assure is a pet care savings program designed to make veterinary, as well as everyday care, more affordable for pet owners. Through a network of participating veterinarians, PetAssure customers save 25 percent on all veterinary products and services. Members can also save 50 percent on pet supplies and other services. This service is not an insurance program. For more information, look to www.petassure.com.

Vision

Our eyes are irreplaceable. It makes sense that we should take care of them. Regular eye exams, use of prescription lenses—glasses or contacts—and even eye exercises are important. With the increasing use of computers, ophthalmologists warn that our eyes are at risk from the intensity of use and the continual focusing on small images. Vision coverage is a wise addition to a basic hospitalization plan.

Other

There are other kinds of insurance benefits that can be provided to employees that don't relate to the body or physical health at all. Consider group automobile insurance or prepaid legal coverage. When you get creative, you can even go so far as to provide insurance protection for such far-out exposures as the weather during a scheduled vacation period. Yes, there are insurance companies that will cover such things. This kind of benefit may seem a little outrageous at first, until you realize the fun—and positive benefit—that may result from some work in this area.

Pets

A few years ago, people laughed at the idea of pet insurance. Now a number of companies do a pretty good business providing insurance coverage direct to pet owners and as a group benefit through employers. Other companies offer discounts to help reduce the cost of owning a pet.

PROVIDE ADOPTION SUPPORT

Some couples are not able to have children biologically and want to adopt. Provide legal support services as an alternative to the medical coverage a family would receive if an employee or spouse gave birth. When the adoptive baby is brought home, offer the same parental leave time as that available after childbirth.

ARRANGE FOR ANNUAL PHYSICAL EXAMINATIONS

Healthcare professionals recommend annual physical examinations. These occasions give the family doctor an opportunity to thoroughly check patients to be sure they're in good health, detect early warning signs, and offer advice that may contribute to better health and better living. If the company can pay for the exam, or a part of it, that's certainly appreciated. Employers can also support this important checkup by giving the worker time off with pay to visit the doctor.

If you were going to adopt a child, wouldn't you like 12 weeks paid leave? You can get it from the same company that offers 26 weeks of pregnancy leave and pays for childcare while employees are away at industry conferences. The company is PC Connection, a New Hampshire-based mail order distributor of computers, that employs over 800 happy people.

The open leadership style of Founder/CEO Patricia Gallup is a significant factor in the company's success. She likes to run a tight operation so she can change direction quickly—the nimble, agile model for successful companies of the future. The company has no trouble attracting workers. Why? Competitive wages and full health benefits—even for part-timers. When a housing shortage made it difficult for her to recruit, Gallup initiated a program to build homes and sell them to employees for $40,000 below cost. Employees got free snow tires and windshield wipers so they could safely navigate New Hampshire's winter roads.

Other innovative benefits? Workers can take a one-month leave for any reason, such as caring for elderly family members. How about free turkeys at Thanksgiving, ski jaunts, casino nights, and hiking trips? Even all-expense paid vacations to the Bahamas are not unheard of. The most productive salesperson can earn a cruise to Cancun and Gallup pays a $1,000 cash bounty for attracting a new employee. "Employees are customers, too," says Gallup, "so we have to exceed their expectations." Result: a 96 percent employee retention rate. And there's a boomerang component: of those who do leave the company, about 10 return each year.[6]

WELLNESS PROGRAMS

There's a strong movement under way today to become—and stay—more physically fit. More people are concerned about nutrition, exercise, stress management, and avoiding habits like smoking or consumption of alcoholic beverages. Employers, as they become sensitive to the needs and interests of their workers, are finding ways to support employee initiatives. In other cases, the employer actually initiates the higher attention to wellness, encouraging the employee to invest more time and attention in keeping his or her body in shape.

While not all employees buy into this wellness movement, those who do really appreciate the interest and support of their employers. That support comes in many forms, varying from company to company and even among groups of employees within companies. The motivation of the employer varies as well, with some genuinely interested in responding to their people and some also seeking ways to better manage insurance premiums. Whatever the rationale, more employers are investing in wellness.

> The Taylor Group, an applications service provider and solutions integrator in Bedford, New Hampshire, believes in taking care of its people with annual flu shots, CPR training, tuition reimbursement, career development training, and a career development and CD-ROM library. In addition, other services are offered throughout the year. For instance, after the company meeting in February, massage therapists are available for the employees.

Offer a Corporate Fitness Center

To support physical well-being, companies encourage employee fitness. A wide range of employers have installed exercise equipment within their facilities. These areas are available 24 hours a day in some environments, restricted in others. In some places, there is minimal equipment—some weight machines, a treadmill, perhaps a stair climber. Other companies have large areas devoted to exercise equipment and even provide saunas and whirlpools.

Some companies employ physical trainers to work with their employees—not just executives, but all people who work for the organization. These trainers, sometimes employees and sometimes outside contractors, coach individuals in their physical fitness regimens and conduct aerobics classes before, during, and after working hours.

Subsidize a Health Club Membership

Employers anxious to support employee fitness purchase memberships in health clubs or fitness centers in the community. This practice has been around for a while as an executive perk, but is now being offered to any employee who will commit to some sort of regimen of exercise. Some companies don't even ask for a commitment to use the benefit, but offer access as a benefit for all.

There are chains of fitness facilities such as World Gym and Gold's Gym, as well as a wide range of smaller chains, franchises, or independent operators. These providers are usually receptive to discounted fee arrangements for corporations or groups. Taking advantage of these opportunities, an employer can help employees without having to invest in acquiring or maintaining its own facilities.

As an added benefit, professional physical trainers are of course available at these public facilities and are happy to work with people whose fees are paid by their employer. Many fitness centers or health clubs have massage therapists on staff or available for appointments on a call-in basis. Massage therapy can be an extra benefit—available to all, based on performance on the job or in the gym or accessible at a discounted group rate.

Some employers consider an employee's physical fitness to be the employee's business, and not an area an employer should even be involved with. A company does not have to become very deeply involved to make a difference for the workers. Employees sincerely appreciate full financial support of fitness programs, but some kind of a subsidy could be just as effective. There is no one right way to relate to employee fitness.

> Many employers now provide fitness facilities for their employees. Sara Lee Knit Products, in Winston-Salem, North Carolina, offers a 24-hour fitness center, health screenings, classes for smoking cessation, weight loss programs, and massage therapy. Oppenheimer Funds Services in Englewood, Colorado, and the Pittsburgh, Pennsylvania Airport have workout facilities for employees. Merck Pharmaceuticals has an outdoor parcours trail at its Elkton, Virginia, plant.

Membership in a health club is the perk most job seekers want from their next employer, according to a Lee Hecht Harrison survey of 1,058 outplaced managers. "Given a wish list of discretionary benefits including use of a company car, concierge services, and tuition reimbursement, the greatest number of respondents (58 percent) indicated they would like to have a health club membership in their new job. Flextime was a close second, desired by 57 percent of respondents. But, when asked which they actually expected to receive, just 8 percent said health club membership. Only 24 percent expect flextime."[7]

Justice Telecom supplements the cost of the membership in the upscale Spectrum Health Club, located across the street from their headquarters in Culver City, California. The employees appreciate the opportunity to work out during lunch or after work without traveling a long distance. In the LA area, where Justice is located, traveling a long distance is time-consuming.

Encourage Good Nutrition

Some employers emphasize nutrition as a vital part of any employee wellness program. Many company cafeterias offer healthy meal options and more meetings are including health bars and fruit for breaks instead of the more traditional pastries, cookies, pretzels, sodas, and chips.

Located in Rye, New York, cataloger Lillian Vernon provides her employees with the monthly services of a nutritionist to help them stay healthy.

Some companies contract with professional nutritionists to come to the workplace on a scheduled basis to meet with interested employees—in group or individual settings. In other cases, employers subsidize or cover all costs of employees working with nutritionists, just as if they were working with doctors or physical therapists. The actual work may be done at the workplace, at the nutritionist's office, or even in the employees' homes.

Provide Wellness Training

Through the company training department, employees in many companies can take classes in time management, stress management, and similar subjects that help them better manage themselves and the environment around them. Using the resources of the American Cancer Society, many companies sponsor smoking cessation programs for their employees and members of the employees' families.

Employee Assistance Programs (EAPs) in many companies provide personal, confidential support for individual employees. Trained counselors and specialists, usually outside contractors rather than company employees, help workers with alcoholism, substance abuse, family problems, emotional difficulties, and a host of other circumstances requiring outside intervention.

> One of the ways in which the coffee chain Starbuck's attracts top-notch part-time employees is by offering them health insurance. One of the employees told us that this insurance benefit is one of the important reasons why he works there. He also likes the fact that he receives one pound of coffee per week!

PROMOTE SPECIAL BENEFITS

Part of what differentiates one company from another are the special, unique benefits that are offered employees. The impact is greatest when the benefits specifically relate to the needs and interests of the employees of the granting company, rather than benefits that are offered just because the company down the street offers them. Obviously, if you know your people well, you can tailor benefits for them. This approach is particularly successful when you involve employees in the design of the benefits package.

Who should receive benefits? Until relatively recently, benefits were an entitlement limited to full-time employees. This policy is changing substantially with the increase in the number of part-time employees and people working flexible hours. Enlightened employers, sensitive to the competitive advantage of offering benefits to all workers, are including part-timers in the distribution. Some companies grant full benefits to part-timers, while others provide partial benefits or allow part-timers to contribute something to be able to receive a full-time benefit. With the many variations about how benefits are allocated, there is certainly no right way to manage these arrangements. Each employer must decide what is best.

Some benefits, including many that will be discussed below, can be granted to contract workers as well as salaried employees.

With the increase in temporary workers, leased employees, and outside contractors, employers should be sensitive to the relationship the company has with these valuable people.

Discount Pricing

If your company provides goods and services to consumers, it may be possible to arrange discounts for employee purchases. The traditional way company products have been offered is through a company store or a company-owned outlet store. Not only are employees able to purchase merchandise at a substantial discount, they take pride in using the company's products and telling others about them. Retailers and some distributors can make merchandise available at significant savings, making working for them a value just from the money saved.

Employers who provide services—such as auto service, tours, telephone or Internet access service, household maintenance, entertainment, or dry cleaning can offer those services to employees at little or no cost to the company. Even though the cost is minimal to the company, the employees place a high value on the benefit because of what those services would cost if they were not able to enjoy employee discounts. Remember: Value is determined by the perceptions of employees, not by what benefits cost!

Logo Apparel and Items

Company products and services are an easy benefit source for employers interested in offering creative benefits to its workers. This gesture can be taken a step further by offering workers an opportunity to purchase apparel and other appropriate items with the company name and/or logo imprinted. Since the exposure gained by people wearing the company logo clothing is good advertising—for people to buy the company's products and for people to consider working for the company—employers can write off some of the cost as advertising or promotional expense. Why, workers might be able to purchase jackets, for instance, cheaper than they could buy similar items at retail stores. Some logo clothing and promotional items can even be given to employees as gifts.

Trade with Other Employers

If your company doesn't produce goods and services that might be valuable to your employees, explore bartering arrangements with local customers. For instance, if you manufacture store fixtures, your employees probably won't have much need for what you sell. However, they might find wonderful value in the products sold by the stores who are the company's customers. The manufacturer can arrange discounts or credits for its employees to purchase from a local outlet.

Let your imagination loose and you will come up with all sorts of ideas of things you can do. For more ideas and a deeper understanding of this strategy, we recommend the book *Streetfighting* by Jeff Slutsky. One of Jeff's ideas is to create a coupon book for your employees with coupons from area merchants interested in attracting your employees as customers.

SUPPORT LOCAL EVENTS OR ATTRACTIONS

There are wonderful opportunities to support local events or attractions in your community. Many companies already arrange discount tickets for amusement parks and similar venues—places such as SeaWorld, Six Flags, and the like. Discounted admissions can be a great benefit for families. Company parties at these venues can be a lot of fun, and can really strengthen bonding at the same time.

Roger once delivered a seminar at a corporate conference of Ben & Jerry's Ice Cream franchisees. During his work with these fine people, he met the distributor serving the area where our offices are located in Greensboro, North Carolina. Trading some books, tapes, and consulting time with the distributor, Roger arranged for some of that delicious ice cream to be delivered to our offices for our employees to take home. Needless to say, our people were absolutely delighted with the special benefit they received—especially because instead of delivering 8 pints per month, as arranged, 80 pints arrived at one time!

At The Herman Group, we purchase the popular annual *Entertainment Book* filled with coupons from restaurants, movies, and attractions. For $25 or $30 (ask about discounts if you have a large employee population), you give people a gift that will last all year. The members of our team really appreciate the coupon book because they use it to have a good time less expensively.

Look for opportunities to support your community and do good things for your people at the same time. For example, community theater groups are comprised of local people who act, prepare the scenery, sell tickets and refreshments, and do all the other tasks involved in mounting a theatrical production. Employers who purchase tickets for their people to attend the shows contribute to the community and to the cultural experience of their employees. The same philosophy applies to community sports teams, community festivals, and similar causes worthy of corporate support.

> At the Herman Group, we buy annual symphony subscriptions. When Roger and Joyce are unable to attend—which is most of the time—the employees take turns attending the concerts.

Many employers purchase box seats or lease lounges at stadiums and arenas. The seats are used for entertaining customers or as perks for executives. For a modest additional investment, those same employers could purchase blocks of tickets that could be used by their employees, families, and even friends (who may be prospective employees).

Don't overlook the opportunities available to you in the sports benefits area just because your company isn't in a major-league team's city. Minor league baseball and hockey can provide high-level excitement and fun, and you may find corporate prices exceedingly reasonable.

SUPPLEMENT PUBLIC TRANSPORTATION

In some areas, getting to work is not such an easy proposition. In urban areas, public transportation is usually easily accessible in central areas of the community. Unfortunately, the bus lines or train lines may not extend to the suburban or exurban locations where many of the jobs are. Savvy employers provide supplemental transportation from the end of the public service to the workplace. This service makes it possible for a more diverse workforce to be employed and provides a valuable public benefit.

Other employers provide van pools, buses or other arrangements for people to share rides to work.

EXPAND SPECIAL SERVICES

Creative employers design benefits that may stretch the imagination, but meet the needs of employees. The only limitation is the imagination. We've seen an exciting variety of services, benefits, and conveniences for their people. Here are some examples to stimulate your thinking.

Dry cleaning pickup and delivery service is offered by a number of large corporations. For example, employees at Allstate Insurance in Northbrook, Illinois, can bring their dry cleaning to a branch of a local dry cleaning service located on a retail concourse in the company's offices. Other larger employers may find local dry cleaners eager to work with them. If you're a smaller employer, don't let that stand in your way. Dry cleaners are usually happy to provide pickup and delivery service to your place of business no matter how many employees you have.

Other services that lend themselves to being provided on-site are shoe repair (or just shoe shining), manicures, neck and shoulder massages, and barber and beauty services. It may not make sense to have these services available every day, but once a week might be appropriate. Some companies, such as automotive oil change and lubrication services, have established regular services where they go from company to company on a set schedule to serve employees on-site.

If your company has a cafeteria, the kitchen staff could prepare ready-to-heat (or microwave) meals for employees to take home for family dinner. This is a benefit that saves time for employees, keeps food from going to waste,

> Employees of the Wilton Conner Packaging Corporation in Charlotte, North Carolina, enjoy the benefit of an on-site laundry service. The company employs people to operate washers and dryers on the company premises. Employees bring their dirty clothes to work and go home in the evening with clean, folded clothes. You may not be able to provide this service in your company's facilities, but there are laundry services associated with Laundromats™ and dry cleaners that may provide a similar benefit for your employees.

> The law firm of English & Gloven in San Diego provides manicures monthly for all employees. 1-800-FLOWERS brings in massage therapists to relax their heavily worked employees around busy times—such as Mother's Day and Valentine's Day. The shoulder massages are really appreciated.

and enables workers to get nutritious meals at a fraction of the cost they may pay on the outside. Note: this could be a terrific boon for welfare-to-work parents, working moms, and single parents.

Through EmployeeSavings.com, Microsoft, Nordstrom, 3M, Northwest Airlines, and others have initiated programs that enable workers to buy discounted products and services at their desktop computers. Workers can purchase groceries, movie tickets, home loans, and other products and services—specially priced for company employees—without leaving their workstations. It's a convenience strategy. Even though a little bit of productivity may be eroded, the time and hassle saved makes the employee happy and less stressed. Online shopping sites are customized for each employer—and there are no fees charged to the employee or the employer to use the shopping service. Third-party software producers charge the retailers who want to make their goods and services available to this market.[8]

Local auto service companies are always happy to get more customers. It's important for them to keep their garages full and their mechanics productive. Arrange for them to offer pickup and delivery service for employees who need mechanical services such as a tune-up, brake work, or new tires.

Other services that can be provided, even with professionals coming on-site at scheduled times to meet with employees, include financial planning, legal services, and accounting. These types of services can be used by a number of employees who might normally have to take time off from work to meet with their advisors. Arranging for this kind of vendor to be conveniently on-site on a scheduled basis makes it unnecessary for many employees to take time off from work to take care of personal business.

EmployeeSavings.com is endorsed by the Employee Services Management Association, a national association that can help you decide what services to offer and where to source those services.

Note that an employer cannot require employees to use the services of particular providers, nor can they deny workers time off to take care of their own business. However, making these services available on-site could help make life a little more convenient and manageable for those employees who choose to use them.

TIME OFF

Survey results confirm that an increasing number of workers want more time off to take care of themselves, their families, and all the little errands that need to be done. When asked if they'd rather have more cash or time off, time-challenged workers are voting for the time off.

Longer Time Off

Colleges and universities for years have offered sabbaticals to their professors. After teaching for a number of years, the instructors can take some time to learn, grow, travel, or try something different. Corporations can do the same thing, and a number of them are. There are many variations on this theme—some pay for the time off, considering it to be a learning experience that will help the employee become that much more effective. Others will pay a stipend or some sort of subsidy during extended vacations. Another approach is to continue benefits while the employee is away from work— paid by the company or by the employee, or simply to hold the job for the employee's return.

BE SENSITIVE TO TWO-INCOME FAMILIES

According to the Bureau of the Census, only 17 percent of households conform to the traditional model of a wage-earning dad, a stay-at-home mom, and one or more children (1997 data). The percentage of married couple/dual income households has doubled, up now to 60 percent. Dual career couples comprise 45 percent of today's workforce.

Intel began offering sabbaticals in 1969, when the company was founded. Employees who take sabbaticals have an opportunity to re-energize; those who are not on sabbatical have an opportunity to take on new challenges by performing some of the duties normally performed by the re-charging employees. Microsoft also offers sabbaticals—as a reward for high-performing employees. Hallmark sponsors team sabbaticals, where 3–10 people take some time off to study, learn, and develop new creative skills. American Express allows employees to take a year of paid leave for community service after 10 years of service. Dupont employees can take a year of unpaid leave, but keep their health benefits. McDonald's offers 8 weeks of paid leave to full-time workers after 10 years of service.

These dual-income families have more money coming in, but the situation is not all happiness and glee. Time management can be a major challenge—in managing child care responsibilities or spending time with each other. Balancing work and personal lives can cause serious stress and conflict in a marriage; who yields in a busy schedule to go home early and take care of the kids? What happens when a spouse gets a job offer out of town and the other partner doesn't want to move?

A major solution is a more flexible schedule, coupled with more family leave time. Company-sponsored childcare can be a major stress-reliever. This caring can be extended significantly by empowering supervisors to exercise flexibility and sensitivity when dealing with an employee who is a dual-income spouse.

Care for the Trailing Spouse

When hiring a new employee who has a working spouse, offer to help find employment for the trailing spouse. Appreciating that the spouse might still be working while the employee is starting a new job and trying to get resettled, offer other kinds of assistance that may be needed. Some possibilities include gathering information on schools, doctors, and other healthcare providers, house-hunting, and simple information about how to get around in the new community. Think of this service as hiring a family, not just an employee. Your caring will make the family feel more welcome, feel more kindly toward the employer, and be more supportive of the new employee on the new job. Stress will be lower, assimilation easier, and productivity higher.

Dependent Care

Employer care for dependents began with childcare, but has expanded to serve other dependents of employees. This care can be provided by the employer with employer-paid staff. This approach is rife with potential problems, and most employers avoid it. A different approach is to contract with one or more outside vendors to provide the service, on company premises or at convenient off-site locations. A third alternative is to provide subsidies to employees to make their own arrangements. In supporting this design, employers maintain lists of recommended or approved care facilities.

Established as an employee benefit, childcare, and similar services can be furnished or supported with before-tax dollars. Careful design of programs can produce tax savings benefits for employees challenged with the care of loved ones.

Childcare

More and more employers offer childcare for their workers. Some of these programs offer the care in company facilities, either staffed by company employees or, more likely, by outside professionals such as KinderKare or LaPetite. In other cases, the care center is off-site, operated solely for the employer or a consortium of employers.

Some employers support their working parents with a subsidy, allowing the families to place the child in a facility that suits their needs. In many cases, the company limits support to approved facilities, but this is not always the case. Other employers simply provide a referral service for parents.

> LaPetite operates a large childcare facility at Opryland Hotel in Nashville, Tennessee. The Child Development Center is open around the clock to accommodate employees at this convention hotel, known for being the largest hotel in the United States outside Las Vegas. The childcare facility serves 350 children. The hotel subsidizes rates on a sliding scale so that the most any employee pays is 80 percent of the normal rate charged by LaPetite.

Occasional Childcare

Employees with school-age children face two challenges that could force them to take time off from work to care for children. One occasion is when a child is ill; the other circumstance is when the children are not in school because of a holiday not granted to workers or a teacher in-service training day. Weather problems can also cause parents to miss work to watch their kids. If schools are closed, someone has to assume responsibility for the students.

Employers, concerned about keeping as many workers as possible on the job, make arrangements for the care of employees' children. Hospitals and clinics, even company facilities in large enough organizations, can care for sick children while their parents are working.

When children of employees at John Hancock Insurance or Ellis Memorial Hospital have a day off from school—for a teachers' workday or a holiday their parents don't get, the company provides age-appropriate field trips. Parents pay $20 for the "Kids-to-Go" program, which covers all activities for the day. For parents with family incomes under $30,000, scholarships are available.

At BankBoston, the number of employees registered to use the company's Snowy Day program is growing each year. More than 400 employees are signed up to take their children to a safe respite on snow days when schools close. The program is offered at seven BankBoston locations in Massachusetts, Rhode Island, and Connecticut and is free to all 16,000 employees.

At the corporate office in Boston, the Snowy Day program is held in a big, bright conference center on the 35th floor. While BankBoston provides the materials for activities, crafts, and games, as well as a VCR, television, and snacks, the actual oversight of the program is managed by Bright Horizons Family Solutions, Cambridge, Massachusetts.

Another alternative, depending on the employee's job responsibilities, is to arrange for the employee to work at home when the children are there. This need-based telecommuting allows the parent to be close by, yet still able to complete at least a partial productive workday.

Backup Childcare

When regular childcare plans don't work, parents are faced with a serious problem. Things happen—a caregiver might be ill, on vacation, or could simply quit. If the parents don't have backup arranged, they'll probably have to miss work to take care of their child(ren). According to the Families and Work Institute in New York, working parents are confronted with this challenge about 3.6 times per year. Clients of ChildrenFirst—more than 200 leading corporations in a wide range of industries—report that their employees use the company's backup centers an average of six times per year. ChildrenFirst serves more than 20,000 registered children in six metropolitan across the country. You can learn more about them at www.childrenfirst.com.

Human resource executives and childcare experts say backup childcare is a cost-effective strategy that seems to be working. Absenteeism is decreased and productivity is increased, and the benefit can be a powerful tool to recruit and retain desired employees. A Hewitt Associates study of 1,020 companies in 1997 revealed that 85 percent of the companies offered childcare benefits and, of those, 15 percent offered backup care. Compare those numbers with the same study in 1992: 74 percent of 1,026 companies offered childcare and only 6 percent of them offered backup care.[9]

Eldercare

The "sandwich" generation is keenly aware of the need to care for elderly parents. Reluctant to simply "store" their loved ones in a nursing home or retirement village, children often move the parents in with them or provide support for them in their own homes. Sometimes the elderly will live in a retirement community of some sort, but receive close care from their loved ones—who are your employees. Problems could require hours or days away from work.

Following guidelines similar to those applied to childcare, an increasing number of employers are providing eldercare. In some cases, the elderly and the young children are in the same or side-by-side facilities. For a short time during the day, the generations are mixed, bringing joy to all.

Special Cases

If any of your employees are caring for dependents who are disabled in any way, there may be a need for special provisions. Unusual and unexpected care needs arise from time to time. They often need extra time to take care of life details that must be addressed. Be sensitive to needs of your employees who may need just a little more flexibility.

Pet Care

An estimated 58.2 million (58.9 percent) of US households owned one or more companion pets in 1996. Of these households—each with at least one working person—45.7 percent owned dogs, cats, or both. The pet cat population at 59 million surpasses the canine count of 52.9 million. Dogs are still more popular: 4.2 million more American households own a dog rather than a cat. Bird ownership has soared to 12.6 million, with at least one bird owned by 4.6 million households in 1996. Other pet counts include 5.7 million rabbits and ferrets, 4.8 million rodents (guinea pigs, hamsters, gerbils), 3.5 million reptiles, and 55.6 million fish.[10]

So: millions of employees have pets, and regard them as being at least as important as children. One employee we interviewed really loves and appreciates his dog. "I don't have to buy my dog clothes, take him places after school, or struggle to get him to clean his room. I get plenty of love, and no back-talk."

Whenever we mention "doggie daycare" in our speeches and seminars, we get chuckles from our audiences. Unusual? Yes. Outlandish and ridiculous? No. Employees who own pets often treat them with the same level of love, care, and concern as parents treat their children. This level of attention is even stronger when the pet owners don't also have children at home. The pet is like a child to them. If a pet is ill, they'd rather be home with the animal than miles away fulfilling employment responsibilities.

Leaving a pet alone in a house while working all day can be disturbing for some owners. It's lonely, quiet, boring, a sad situation, not just for the puppy or kitty, but from the perspective of the worker who abandons the animal for 8–10 hours or more as well. Placing the pet in a happy, active, loving environment for the workday is a much better alternative.

When the facilities and environment are right, some employers invite their employees to bring

---

Washington, D. C.'s first daycare center for dogs, Dog-ma, opened its doors in September 1998. The 7,000 square foot facility, located less than a mile from the U.S. Capitol and the Supreme Court, is open weekdays from 7:30 A.M. to 8:00 P.M., offering "cageless" service. Dog-ma screens prospective clients (the dogs, that is) for temperament, suitability, health, and neutering. www.dog-ma.com.[11]

When Justice Telecom, at one time the fastest-growing privately held company in the country, first opened its doors more than six years ago, its staff members were young and many did not have children. But they did have pets. A number of them had dogs that were just as important to them as other people's children.

On-site pet care at Justice was the brainchild of

their pets to work. Others provide separate care facilities adjacent to the workplace. Company-paid or contract workers stay on duty to care for employee pets, feed them, exercise them, and protect them. Sometimes these arrangements are made by the employer directly. Other arrangements include employee co-operatives, and some companies contract with nearby boarding kennels for support services.

When employees travel on company business, some employers pay for care of pets while the employee is away. The funding could pay for someone to come to the employee's home to feed and care for the pets, walk the dog, and so forth. Or, the employee can take the pet to an approved boarding kennel for company-paid care during the absence.

With the closeness that develops between many pets and their people, it's understandable that some employees would like to take their pets to work. In some work environments, where it's safe—for the animal and humans—this can be encouraged. In most cases, when pets are brought to work, they stay with their humans in the humans' work areas. In other situations, employers are providing doggie day care.

their Chief Operating Officer, Leon Richter. Richter spoke with Carol Schwartz, Justice's director of human resources. Carol went to president David Glickman, who allowed her to create a dog run and hire a staff member.

Due to a reorganization, Justice needed the space and had to eliminate the dog run. Don't worry: Justice employees still enjoy bringing their pets to work with them. But now, the pets stay under their owners' desks. At lunch, the dog owners take their pets for walks in nearby grassy areas. Carol believes that the mere presence of pets in the office "relieves stress" in their intense environment.

Pets are welcome at work at Netscape, though there are some strict policies. Dogs may not eat each other's food or have more than two indoor accidents. They must be considerate, quiet, and congenial. If a dog misbehaves three times, the owner must take it to obedience school. The owner must show human resource professionals proof that the dog has graduated from obedience school.

Ben & Jerry's and Iams, the pet food manufacturer in Dayton, Ohio, also have pet-friendly policies. Iams goes even further. Kersee, a golden retriever, was named vice president of canine communications and given an office near the reception area where she can greet visitors.[12]

PART-TIMERS ARE PEOPLE, TOO

The practice for years was not to give benefits to part-time employees. Many companies sought to hire part-timers instead of full-timers wherever they could to avoid the benefits costs. All that has changed. A trend towards providing part-timers benefits began a few years ago when, in the tight labor market, employers began paying partial costs for part-timers and/or allowing part-timers to purchase all or part of their benefits.

The 23,000 part-time employees at Marriott may participate in a 401(k) plan, earn paid time-off, and join in a stock purchase plan. Employees at Deloitte & Touche who work 20 hours or more a week get the same medical, dental, and other benefits as full-timers. Burger King employees at corporate headquarters who work less than 30 hours a week can get medical benefits, but at a higher premium. After two years with Wal-Mart, part-timers become eligible for holiday pay, medical care, 401(k), and a scholarship program.[13]

Now part-timers have become as scarce and dear as full-time employees and employers are responding with attractive benefit packages for them. In a number of organizations, part-time and full-time employees get the same benefit package.

Notes

1. "Americans@Work," Jeffrey L. Seglin, *Inc.* Magazine, June 1998, page 91.
2. Retaining Employees a Top Concern Study Report, American Management Association, 1999.
3. "Employers Expanding Stock Options to All," *HR Magazine*, October 1999.
4. "Just Deserts," Patricia M. Carey, *Working Woman*, December/January 1999, page 72.
5. "GTECH to offer domestic partners healthcare benefits," Nora Lockwood, *The Providence Journal*, December 7, 1999.
6. "Leadership for the Millennium," Esther Wachs Book, *Working Woman* Magazine, March 1998.
7. Len Strazewski, "Health Club Memberships Wanted," *Human Resource Executive* Magazine, November 1999.
8. "Workers bag new perk with shopping on the job," Stephanie Amour, *USA Today*, November 16, 1999.
9. "Emergency Breaks," Charlotte Adams, *Human Resource Executive* Magazine, May 4, 1999.

10. American Veterinary Medicine Association's Center for Information Management. Additional information is contained in the *US Pet Ownership and Demographic Sourcebook*, available for $79.50 to the general public. Call (847) 925-8070, extension 297 for ordering or more information.
11. "Day Care Goes to the Dogs," Melanie Goldman, *Fast Company*, July-August 1999, page 78.
12. "It's a Pet's World," Rhonda K. Miller, Human Resource Executive, June 5, 1998.
13. "Part-timers reap benefits of tight market," Stephanie Amour, *USA Today*, November 1, 1999.

MAKING A DIFFERENCE

A shift in social values is beginning to infiltrate corporate culture. A sense of legacy, a word coming into much more common usage, is inspiring people to want to make a difference in the world around them. Some people focus on their local community, while others look at a bigger picture including making the world a better place.

An increasing proportion of our population feels that we have a responsibility to make this a better world. Both individuals and corporations should contribute time, money and in-kind goods and services toward this objective. This feeling has become much stronger in recent years—a sort of evolution of consciousness.

People want to make a difference for their families, their communities, the world. Giving of ourselves to help others raises our self-esteem. It makes us feel good about ourselves. We feel good when we work with employers who invest in the community and the world.

There are a number of worthwhile alternatives for corporate citizenship. At the local level, there are opportunities for economic development, downtown fix-up, kids programs, activities for the elderly, cultural events and much, much more. Chambers of commerce provide leadership, but so do Rotary Clubs, Kiwanis and other worthwhile organizations.

Beyond the local level, there are regional and national opportunities for involvement. Save the Children, American Red Cross and Boy and Girl Scouts of America are just a few of the service organizations with which you can become involved. Individuals and companies can also provide assistance for victims of floods, hurricanes, and other disasters. On a global level, corporations support literacy programs, programs to feed the hungry, and efforts to stop the exploitation of children. Foundations, international relief organizations, religious groups, and a wide range of civic and professional organizations help facilitate personal and corporate support for those in need.

SIMPLE WORKS

You don't have to save the world single-handedly to make a positive difference. Helping one organization or cause, one family, or even one person can make the world a better place. So, a word of caution as we begin this chapter. The concept of making the world a better place, of making a difference, doesn't require dramatic, save-the-world strategies that drain the company's resources. Little things count, too.

Traditionally, corporations have contributed money—always needed—to support selected causes. This kind of support is valuable; corporate funding really makes a difference. The key to making the outreach important for being an Employer of Choice is that the employees know about the contributions, agree with them, and that the workers feel good because they're being made by their employers. Generous employers are appreciated by their employees because people feel that the profits

> Each department of Arizona Mail Order, one of the largest mail order companies in the country, adopts a needy family from the local community during the December holiday season. The teams from each of the departments hold in-company bake sales and do other things to raise money. Then team members shop together for food and gifts for their family. On Christmas Eve, the members of the department, as a group, deliver the goodies to the needy family. This project is completed at no cost to the company; it's all self-funded by the employees.

> Uni-Mail List Corp., in New York City, rents mailing lists. In fact, they are one of the leading mailing list brokers in the country. Instead of sending Christmas gifts to clients and suppliers, at holiday time Uni-Mail sends a large donation to Save the Children. The company includes a small note in its holiday cards informing recipients of the gift.

they help earn make a difference in the world.

While direct funding will continue to be important, a trend now gaining strength is to more intimately involve the people who work for the company in the charities and causes it supports. More than just "sweat equity," the shift is to engaging heart and soul in the process of reaching out. One approach is to encourage employees to volunteer, perhaps giving them time from work (sometimes significant paid time off). Another approach is for employees to support civic work as part of their jobs.

Remember that your people want to feel that they're making a difference, so look for ways to emphasize the human involvement component of your community outreach.

> Burrell Professional Labs, the world's largest network of portrait and wedding photographic labs, has long been considered the nation's premiere photo finisher for professional photographers. Don Burrell, president, believes in sharing the wealth his company earns. To mark his 40th year in business, he pledged $40,000 to the Professional Photographers Association Charities. The 1999 beneficiary was the Elizabeth Glaser Pediatric AIDS Foundation. Don founded the Burrell Cancer Institute at the St. Anthony Medical Center in the company's home town of Crown Point, Indiana. He also supported construction of a 30-bed shelter for battered women and their children.

SUPPORT YOUR EMPLOYEES THROUGH CONTRIBUTIONS

Most employers are solicited on a regular and frequent basis by civic organizations. Funds are allocated according to the decisions of an executive committee or similar group. Smaller firms

> Brink's Home Security gives one day off per year to every employee to volunteer in community service. Timberland employees may use up to 40 hours of paid time per year for volunteer work. Other companies encourage employees to volunteer four hours a week and allow flexibility in working hours to accommodate people attending meetings or providing direct services in civic organizations.

have no budget and no controls, simply responding to whoever appears at the door with a hand out.

Here's an idea for your consideration. Get your employees—all of them—actively involved. Determine how much money you will allocate for contributions during the year. Divide that amount by the number of employees you have. Then invite each employee, sometime during the year, to designate where his or her portion will go. Ask them not to select any controversial causes like the Pro-Life movement, but to concentrate on organizations that make their community a better place to live.

As the year goes on, employees will decide where they want their share to go—a marathon to fight a disease, United Way, a community park building program, Little League, a scouting program, Red Cross, community theater, or a kids cultural program.

This approach is an exciting win-win proposition. The community wins, the company doesn't have to decide where the money's going, a deserving local cause gets corporate support, and the employee has some power over company resources to do good things.

A side benefit is the sense of empowerment and partnership that the employee experiences.

Community Theater

We like the idea of supporting community theater because the people involved are local citizens working hard to make a difference. Some of your employees may be actors, scenery designers, or otherwise connected to community theater. Sponsorship of a performance, purchasing advertisements in the program, providing in-kind support for scenery or props or buying a block of tickets are ways you can encourage local theater. Here's an idea with a double benefit: purchase blocks of tickets to community theater performances and distribute them to your employees and their families. The theater benefits, and so do your employees and their families. Your people will enjoy an evening or afternoon out, and they'll get a dose of culture, too.

Cultural Events

Most communities have some sort of cultural events that deserve support. Depending on the size of the community, there could be a fairly wide range of theater, music, and art activities. Local organizations producing operatic, theatrical, musical, and artistic events can always benefit from corporate and individual support.

They always need help, from service on a board of directors to people that distribute programs to patrons.

Financial support can be employed in purchasing advertisements in programs, to sponsor performances, or to facilitate community outreach. A donation of funds, and perhaps transportation of equipment, could enable a cultural production to visit local schools so kids can be exposed to culture. This sort of work is particularly important in enhancing the education of disadvantaged children whose schools may not be able to afford the luxury of this sort of program.

> HA-LO Industries, a Chicago-based specialty advertising firm, is known for its charitable work. Each year, the company sends hundreds of underprivileged children to professional sporting events. The HA-LO Kids Heaven program has provided free tickets to Chicago Bulls and Chicago White Sox games for years. Over 2,000 deserving kids benefit from this program each year, attending games with employees of HA-LO.

Sporting Events

Professional sports, semi-professional sports, and amateur sports are all of interest to employees. Various levels of sponsorships are available with most teams. You can purchase blocks of seats, logos, season tickets, or advertising space in programs or stadiums. You can arrange for employees to attend games or purchase tickets to be used by people who might not ordinarily be able to experience a sporting event. If your support is strong enough, you might be able to get players to visit your offices, plant or store to greet employees and customers.

United Way

While United Way is a national effort, the principal work they do takes place in individual communities. Funds are raised—with a lot of corporate help—and distributed to a wide range of carefully monitored community service organizations. With the help of employee volunteers, companies raise money from employee donations and through bake sales and other activities. Companies themselves make healthy contributions.

Some employers are giving their employees a choice of where their annual charitable contributions go. These options include charities offered individually or collectively through America's Charities, Earth Share, Combined Health Appeal, and International Service Agencies. All four together are known as Charities@Work.

The United Way Loaned Executive Program provides a valuable opportunity for corporations to help the community, and it gives executives some valuable learning experience. Under the traditional program, corporate managers or executives are assigned to work for United Way—full-time or part-time—for three months. During the campaign, a loaned executive assumes responsibility for 50–150 accounts—businesses that help raise money.

> Glaxo-Wellcome is a very strong supporter of the United Way Loaned Executive Program. Through the program, they donate two people and sponsor eight in the Triangle United Way in Raleigh, North Carolina. Carolina Power & Light provides one to four people, and Nortel Network contributes one executive each year. In Greensboro, North Carolina, loaned executives may take advantage of a week's training provided as an in-kind contribution from the well-known Center for Creative Leadership, based in the community.

The advantages to the employer include introducing new employees to the business community, giving recently relocated managers an opportunity to build contacts in the new community, and providing a vehicle for a different kind of training and experience. United Way is also able to keep its overhead low so that more of the funds collected go directly to the causes that need the financial support.

About half the participating companies can't afford to spare their executives, so they give a special grant to United Way to fund positions. United Way then uses the money to hire the people it needs to help manage the campaign to achieve community goals.

Most of the organizations that receive United Way funding are abundantly staffed by volunteers. Companies can encourage volunteerism by valuing civic involvement and recognizing such contributions, dedication, and leadership in corporate communications, including newsletters and even advertisements in local newspapers featuring their people working in the community. Some employers grant paid time off, a certain number of hours per week or per month, for employees to volunteer for the United Way agencies themselves.

"For 30 years, United Parcel Service managers have participated in the company's Community Internship Program (CIP). At a cost of millions of dollars to the company, more than 1,000 UPS employees have worked with non-profit organizations in distressed areas such as South Side Chicago and the border town of McAllen, Texas. As many as 40 managers a year serve food at soup kitchens, run bingo games for senior citizens, visit AIDS patients in hospices, and ride with inner-city police officers. They build low-income housing and help disadvantaged men and women find jobs. In the process, they gain new perspectives and learn a lot about the world around them—and about themselves.

Managers who participate in CIP do not volunteer; they're tapped by top-level UPS executives." Upper level managers are selected for what they may gain, and what they may bring to the table. "Once the employees are picked, they're assigned to groups of eight at one of four locations: the Henry Street Settlement in New York City, the South Texas Community Internship in McAllen, the St. Margaret of Scotland Parish in Chicago, and the University of Tennessee at Chattanooga, from which workers can help out in streets of that city and in the mining towns of nearby Appalachia. Prior to leaving, employees receive an information packet and spend about six hours in orientation.

Participating UPS employees receive full pay for the month they are gone and are allowed to go back home for one week-end in the middle of the assignment. They're encouraged to call home during the internship, but not the office. They're asked to keep a journal of their experiences, and many of them share some of the things they did with their co-workers after they came back to work. They are also interviewed by human resources staff about what they learned from CIP and how they might apply that knowledge to their jobs."[1]

Delta Air Lines employees who have been injured and are recuperating can transition back to work by doing some work for such charities as the American Red Cross, United Way, or Children's Miracle Network. The experiment began in the Fall of 1999 at Delta's Salt Lake City, Utah, hub. The policy is mandatory for ground employees and voluntary for flight attendants, a total of about 4,000 workers. Although the idea is meeting some resistance as we go to press, it could be a valuable pioneering effort.[2]

Fund-Raising

Walkathons, bike-a-thons, and even rock-a-thons (rocking chairs) are great vehicles for raising money to fight diseases or support other worthwhile causes. Corporate sponsorships include funding, donations, in-kind support to promote and manage the event, and gifts (usually promotional items) for participants.

Many companies recruit a number of their employees to participate as a group. Walking a number of miles can be a lot more fun when you are in the company of a group of friends or co-workers. Some companies represented by groups of employees will provide their participants with matching shirts or caps. The similarity of clothing and the shared experience bonds people more closely together. They choose to do this as part of the company they chose to work for. The sense of pride and contribution is evident, and their engaging presence is wonderful promotion for the company being a good place to work.

> Funds are raised to support leukemia research by people running in designated marathons around the country. In 1999, over $61 million was collected this way. On December 12, 1999, $8 million was raised by 3,600 participants in the Honolulu Marathon, a 26.2 mile experience that began with torrential rain and gusty winds, followed by cloudy and humid weather. Of the 26,724 people who started the marathon and the 21,185 who finished, you can believe that those who were running and walking for a cause were most fulfilled. One of them, Sharon Adcock, a professional speaker and a colleague of ours, proudly raised $5,169.60, making her the number one fund-raiser in Los Angeles for this event.

HIGHWAY CLEANUP

Countless employers have adopted sections of highways throughout the country. Their employees periodically walk the sides of the road together, picking up the trash that motorists have thoughtlessly tossed out of their vehicles. The recognition signs placed by the highway department are nice positive publicity for the employer, but the greater benefit is the feeling people get by cleaning up the roadside—and seeing a noticeable difference as a result of their work. A sense of ownership is also available, particularly if your section of highway is on a route frequently used by your employees—"This is our road."

HELPING KIDS

In most communities, you can find wonderful programs designed to help kids—in school and in life. Companies adopt classes, schools, or special groups of students. They provide tutors, special programs, and even guarantee college educations for kids who will stay in school and earn reasonable grades.

Some employers focus on the children of their own employees, providing charter schools and special programs that bond the kids and their parents.

COMMUNITY SERVICE PROJECTS

There always seem to be plenty of things to do in every community. Fix up, paint up, or whole new development projects—the opportunities are there. You can become involved with projects on an ongoing year-round basis, or have special days devoted to making a significant difference.

Your company and its employees may wish to assume partial or full responsibility

Since 1997, Texas Instruments, along with four other Dallas ABC companies, has offered a unique program for employees' children, ages 12–15. Summer of Service gives youngsters the opportunity to work on fun and educational community service projects four days a week, with Fridays reserved for special recreational field trips. Participants worked on projects including painting over graffiti, visiting senior citizens homes, and working at the Dallas Zoo. The eight-week program, which runs from 7 A.M. until 5:30 P.M., can be attended for the entire summer or on a week-to-week basis.

DataTel, Inc., a software developer in Fairfax, Virginia, sells a fully integrated enterprise resource management system that supports every aspect of college and university operations. The 350-employee company enjoys a 13 percent turnover rate in the middle of the suburban Virginia high-tech corridor. An integral part of Datatel's culture is giving back to the community. Every May 1, the company's Founder's Day, employees, family, and friends participate in a community service day. They've remodeled a house, rebuilt trails at a local park, helped with track and field events for Special Olympics, and helped make a child's wish come true through the Make a Wish Foundation. Some employees mentor and tutor students at a local elementary school. Through their Datatel Scholars Foundation, the company has awarded over $1.2 million to more than 1,000 students who are enrolled at their client sites.

for a community facility or event—existing or new. Maybe you could manage a senior citizens center, or even establish one if no such service is available in your area. There might be a lot of work to be done, depending on how big a project you want to tackle. Be sure you have enough resources—human and otherwise—to avoid falling short of expectations.

> At Patrice Tanaka & Company, Inc., a public relations firm in New York, employees are given the day off on Valentine's Day each year. They use this time to show their love for their fellow man by performing community service work.

HABITAT FOR HUMANITY

This international, nonprofit, ecumenical Christian housing ministry seeks to eliminate substandard housing and homelessness from the world. People of all backgrounds to join in partnership to build homes for those who can't afford them. Since 1976, the program has built over 80,000 simple, decent houses in more than 2,000 communities in all 50 states and in 60 other countries. Through volunteer labor and donated materials, Habitat builds and rehabilitates houses with the help of the homeowner (partner) families. Houses are sold to the partner families at no profit, and financed with affordable, no-interest loans. The homeowner's monthly mortgage payments are used to build more homes.

> Hall Ambulance Company serves Kern County and the area around Bakersfield, California. Their distinctive blue and orange vehicles are a welcome sight when there's an emergency; their people are well-trained, efficient, and highly effective at what they do. Owner Harvey Hall believes strongly in community service, so this company is involved. Hall Ambulance employees manage the Bakersfield Independence Day parade every July.

Habitat is not a giveaway program. In addition to a down payment and monthly mortgage payments, homeowners invest hundreds of hours of their own labor—"sweat equity"—into building their Habitat house and the houses of others. See www.habitat.org for more information.

The Habitat for Humanity web site lists more than 60 major corporate sponsors. There are some great opportunities here, including those on a local basis. You don't have to be a corporate giant to make a difference. Check out the matching gift program.

RESPONSE TO EMERGENCIES

When disaster strikes, corporations can be angels for those who have suffered. Some companies will just give because they think it's the thing to do. Others will concentrate their giving in communities where they have facilities or employees. Some concentrate on really taking care of their own employees and their families, reaching out as a corporate family.

CHILDREN'S HEALTH

There are a number of groups that support the health of children in the United States and around the world. The United Nations Children's Emergency Fund (UNICEF) and Operation Smile are two programs that get things done. Operation Smile, founded in 1982, travels to 19 developing countries and the United States with surgeons who treat children with facial deformities. Over 53,000 children have been treated. The organization relies on volunteers and corporate sponsors.

CHILD LABOR LAWS

The recent outcry against child labor has raised an issue that's very important to a lot of people. A number of American companies operate plants in

When Hurricane Floyd caused unprecedented damage and personal loss—mostly from flooding—in North Carolina, corporations sprang to the rescue. Boddie-Noell, an operator of over 330 Hardee's Restaurants and other ventures, is based in Rocky Mount, North Carolina, one of the areas hardest hit by the storm. The company's attention was immediately focused on their people and their communities. During the initial recovery period, the company arranged for two truckloads of critically needed drinking water to be distributed in their home area of Nash and Edgecombe counties.

Next, the attention turned to relief efforts. Company restaurants outside the affected area collected food, clothing, and supplies for affected co-workers and others in their communities. All the stores got involved in fundraising that produced more than $180,000 for flood victims. Throughout this period, the company focused on their employees whose families were displaced by Hurricane Floyd. A home-office team member assumed responsibility for follow through with each family, with care continuing long after the storm was gone. One effort focused on making sure that every child in a displaced family still had a great Christmas. The company's culture was reflected in the corporate and employee response to care for any employee who needed help with an outpouring of love and warmth.

developing countries. While the values in those countries may tolerate or even condone child labor and long hours with low pay even for adults, these values are not consistent with American values about the way children and workers should be treated. Employers of Choice are highly sensitive to the way their employees are treated—anywhere in the world. This concern needs to extend to employees of companies from whom American companies purchase products and services.

ENCOURAGE ENTREPRENEURIAL INITIATIVE

Many Americans place a high value on entrepreneurship, recognizing the strength and benefit of entrepreneurs starting businesses, creating more jobs, and making a difference. Whether those entrepreneurs are based in the United States or in another country, the same principles of support apply. The principles can be learned early in life, then nourished to fruition.

Organizations like Junior Achievement (JA) provide opportunities for you to promote entrepreneurship. Since 1919, JA has educated and inspired young people to help them gain a fundamental understanding of the free enterprise system. Support opportunities range from corporate sponsorships to actually being involved in the classroom in one of the many K–12 educational programs. To learn more, visit www.ja.org.

Some Citibank employees spend vacations as volunteers with Operation Smile. It's a life-changing experience. Warner Lambert sponsored a youth conference to bring together high school and college youth clubs in a number of countries. The company agreed to match funds, dollar for dollar, raised by the youth groups. As an award for their top salespeople, Warner Lambert sponsors a child in the name of top performers.

Levi Strauss, committed to doing business only with companies that share its values, prepared a list of criteria that defines the values they expect in their international manufacturers and suppliers. Companies that want to do business with Levi Strauss are assessed based on their environmental records, ethical standards, health and safety in work and residential facilities, compliance with laws and employment practices. The company insists that there be no physical risks in the workplace and that workers not be exploited in any way.

The Body Shop, a retailer of bath and beauty supplies, is active in the development of ethical, sustainable relationships with suppliers in developing countries. The company concentrates on creating entrepreneurial ventures in areas of the world that are disadvantaged in terms of employment, skill levels, income, education, health care and similar concerns. Working with established organizations within communities, such as farming cooperatives, tribal councils, and groups of women, the company concentrates on providing skills training, participation opportunities and increased income. The Body Shop purchases goods from entrepreneurs that they have helped develop. Everybody wins.

GIFT OF SIGHT

Efforts to help people see better make quite a difference around the world. Just providing glasses for people who might not otherwise have them—because of a lack of access to vendors or the money to purchase them—is significant. Funding operations for those who need medical help to allow them to be able to see takes this work to the miracle level. Imagine being able to see clearly after spending most—or all—of your life without full sight. The Lions Clubs are heavily involved in these efforts internationally, as are a number of corporate and not-for-profit organizations.

You don't have to save the world all by yourself, and, in fact, you don't have to save the whole world at all. Simply look for places in your community—corporate or otherwise—where you can work to make even a small but crucially needed change.

Lenscrafters, a large optical retailer, works with Lions Clubs and reaches out even further through its employees. Optometrists, opticians, and technicians go on missions to other countries to provide eye testing, to grind lenses, fit frames and deliver glasses to those in need. In a two-week mission, working 12 hours a day for seven to nine days, associates can help as many as 13,000 people. Lenscrafters' goal is to provide glasses to one million needy people by 2003.

Notes

1. "Delivering the Good," John Steinbeder, *Sky* Magazine, April 1998.
2. "Recovering Delta workers can aid charities," Chris Woodyard, *USA Today*, September 1, 1999.

GETTING STARTED

Becoming an Employer of Choice may seem like an almost overwhelming challenge. There's so much to do, so much competition, and such a volatile environment in the labor market. While it may seem like a daunting feat, it really isn't that difficult to become an Employer of Choice. Your organization may not be selected to be on one of the Top 10 or Top 100 lists like we see in *Fortune*, *Working Mother*, or *Computerworld* magazines, but you can still be recognized as an Employer of Choice. Most importantly, your organization can become more effective in attracting, optimizing, and holding on to wonderful people who enjoy serving your internal and external customers, and achieving your goals with enthusiasm.

It's fine to set your sights high—aim for some of that national competitive recognition. The competitive positioning may be important in the minds of some prospective employees, but people recognize that competitive programs can be limiting. They're looking beyond all that Top 100 stuff to find employers that will be right for them. Each worker, regardless of background, education, specialty, age, experience, or level, is looking for what's best personally for him or her. Being on a Top 100 list doesn't necessarily mean that an employer is the best place for everyone to work, quite the contrary, in fact. As people determine what they want, they'll seek employers that offer that special and unique combination.

DIFFERENT WORKERS WILL JUDGE EMPLOYERS ON DIFFERENT CRITERIA

There will be some commonalities, some things that most people will want. There will be some unique expectations that will flow from personal obligations, ambitions, and dreams. As each worker creates and refines that personal list of criteria, the choosing process will begin. There will be experimentation as workers check the reality of the employer's image and of the promises made during the hiring process. Some workers will still leave relatively quickly to continue their search for what they want, to make other choices. But, when the hiring process and the engagement process has been done well, people who choose to join you will choose to stay—for all the right reasons.

Your organization is already an Employer of Choice for all the people who work there. You're probably reading this book because while you have strength in your current workforce, the total human resource you have is not sufficient. Too many people come and go. Not enough people come. Some of those who come—and stay—are not high performers. Maybe you're growing and more fine people will be needed in the months and years ahead. You want to become *more* of an Employer of Choice. You want to be recognized in the labor marketplace as an employer who should not be overlooked as high-potential workers consider their options for their next career moves.

The concept of Getting Started almost implies that an employer is at square one. Unless you're a start-up, you already have a culture, a reputation, and a history. You are not starting from scratch, which means you may need to make some significant changes in the way you do business in order to become worthy of recognition as an Employer of Choice.

Getting started will probably mean different things to different organizations. However, there are some common fundamentals that must be part of your formula, part of your process. Let's explore them, and their implications, as you begin your movement to earn the recognition and benefits of becoming an Employer of Choice.

Strategic Issues

Becoming an Employer of Choice is a strategic issue. It's a bottom line issue. The decision to earn the right to be legitimately recognized with this coveted descriptor must be made at the highest levels in the organization. If your senior leaders are not enthusiastic about becoming an Employer of Choice, you're wasting your time. It won't happen in a genuine, complete way; your status will be a sham and a joke. The perceived insincerity could actually backfire, causing more people to choose to leave.

The impetus for change must come from the top leader. As the commitment is passed down through the organization, the concept becomes real, believable, and energized. Without the solid, dedicated leadership of the top executive, no organization can truly be an Employer of Choice. The pieces may be there, but the cohesiveness will not be sustainable.

Before beginning this process, the top executives or managers should sit down to discuss the Employer of Choice concept and what it might mean to the stability, strength, results, and future potential of the organization. During this serious conversation, participants should create an image, a description, of what being an Employer of Choice means to them. How does it look? What will life in that kind of company be like?

The Nuts and Bolts

Now, let's get down to reality. How would you describe your organization today, relative to your concept of what it would be like for you to be what you envision as an Employer of Choice? How far apart are you, and how far are you from being what you want to be? What will it take to move from where you are to where you want to be? Is it doable? What resources will it take, and are you willing to commit those resources?

These are all strategic questions that must be resolved at the top of the organizational chart before anything else can happen. As part of your evaluation, consider the why question. Why bother investing all the resources that it will take to become an Employer of Choice? Consider these advantages.

Imagine the long-term power, effectiveness, and efficiency of a stable workforce of highly talented and dedicated people with knowledge, experience, understanding, cohesiveness, and continuity. Things get done, with minimal stress, confusion, and waste.

Customers and clients are more comfortable doing business with you. Through longer-term relationships, trust levels increase with a corresponding increase in business. The bottom line becomes stronger and stronger.

WHAT IT ALL MEANS

Becoming an Employer of Choice may be perceived by some as just doing a lot of nice things for employees—the touchy-feely stuff, a paternalistic environment, that sort of thing. It's far more than that—it's a deliberate corporate strategy created out of self-interest. It's certainly good to do well by employees, to do charitable things in the community, and so forth. But, quite frankly, this strategy is implemented from self-interest, recognizing that by becoming an Employer of Choice, you will keep talented people coming in the front door and staying longer than they intended. This strategy is a commitment, not just a temporary Band-Aid™ solution to a labor shortage problem.

The relationship between employers and employees is changing. Today, and certainly in the future, employers will treat workers more like customers—*internal* customers. Many companies

At the close of 1999, the Big Five public accounting firm of Deloitte Touche announced it was stronger than ever, with an 18 percent increase on record earnings. Now in its sixth consecutive year of growth, the firm attributed these results to its ability to hire and retain talented staff. "Deloitte is being recognized increasingly around the world as a leader in its human resources and staff retention strategies, and our results reflect the importance we attach to hiring and making sure we hold onto the best people in the profession," says Jim Copeland, global chief executive officer of Deloitte & Touche Tohmatsu.[1]

A division of Daimler-Chrysler discovered that they were getting correlative results from customer and employee surveys. When the employees were happy, the customer satisfaction scores were high. When the employees weren't happy, the customer satisfaction scores were lower. There was such a correlation that the company decided to stop spending money on customer surveys and concentrate on the employees instead.

treat employees this way already, but too many others just talk about it, and don't really follow through with policy and action. Management rhetoric isn't enough anymore. If you really treat your worker customers as well or better than you treat your buying customers, you'll achieve enviable results.

The conditions that motivate organizations to become Employers of Choice are not limited to the United States or to North America. This fast-changing labor environment is global. Whether you do business globally or not, you will compete with local and global employers for competent, dependable, proficient workers. While you're working within your market arena, be ever sensitive to the bigger picture about what's happening in the international competition for talent.

> The Dutch financial group ABN Amro faces a serious challenge. R. A. Kleyn, general manager of personnel, explains that the company is already receiving noticeably fewer applicants than it did three years ago. The bank is also confronted with the retirement of the Baby Boom generation; over the next ten years, 80 percent of their senior staff will leave. "Employees have actually become clients," Mr. Kleyn observes, "adding a different dimension to personnel policy." The company has become more active in its recruitment work, attracting students while they are still at the University. "Our most important task is to be an 'Employer of Choice,'" Mr. Kleyn explains. "Money is no longer the most important criteria when choosing a job; now factors like career development opportunities top the list."[2]

Getting All Managers Involved

This evaluation and decision process cannot be limited to top management. Once senior leadership has gone through the initial deliberations, managers at all levels must become involved. They may see things differently, and they may have some valuable input to offer. As the organization contemplates making the changes necessary to become an Employer of Choice, all managers, down to the front-line supervisors, must be involved.

In our consulting work, we have a phrase that we use frequently: People support what they help to create. Get all the managers involved in the process of evaluating current conditions, exploring future possibilities, and developing plans to move to a different way of doing business. Earn their support early; it will be invaluable—critical—later.

During this phase of the work, all managers on-board—the chief executive officer, the president, the chief operating officer, and others—must become charismatic leaders. They must assure that the beliefs to which senior management is committed are cascaded down to every level of the organization, with the level of buy-in that will produce desired results during the transformation to Employer of Choice.

Change in Leadership Style

A change in leadership style may be needed. If so, the training, coaching, and mentoring to make this shift happen should start early in the transformation process. A substantial majority of managers and supervisors have been trained in traditional styles of management. This style is relatively directive and autocratic; the boss is clearly in charge. Reinforcement over the years has solidified this approach in many ways. This style worked fine for many years, but it won't work well today and it surely won't work in the future. Supervisors, managers, and many executives must make the shift to be more modern leaders. The difference is considerably more than just semantic.

In Employer of Choice organizations, workers can and will take much more responsibility for themselves and their work. They want to be more accountable, and they want more collaboration with others to get things done. They are reluctant to be closely supervised and are resistant to being micromanaged.

If workers want one type of relationship with their leaders, and management wants another sort of relationship, conflict will inevitably occur. Senior management and human resource professionals will have to resolve these conflicts. The problems will escalate unless they are addressed early. That's why we recommend that leadership training, based on the evolving Employer of Choice corporate culture, be scheduled early in the process. As managers begin practicing the new leadership principles, difficulties will wane and people will start working together in new ways that will support the impending changes.

Leaders need to become facilitators of every individual's high performance. The emphasis will be on the individual, rather than on teams. Focused, supported individuals will then form their own teams, from the inside out, creating a different kind of energized environment that will be highly attractive to workers who are making choices about where they will be.

Don't ignore informal leaders. They can be quite influential and need to brought on-board early. Solicit their ideas for strategies and key people they recommend become involved in the processes of change.

Even as the transformation takes hold and your organization starts to look, feel, and behave like an Employer of Choice, senior leaders must stay involved. During a change process, there is always a feeling of uncertainty until the new ways are firmly in place. People will be watching, checking: is the CEO still in favor of all this? Still involved? The reinforcement and encouragement from the top levels of the company will provide the level of confidence people need to continue forward movement.

Front-Line Supervisors Are Most Critical

Recent research on employee retention, including some great work done by the Corporate Leadership Council, a membership-based research group in Washington, D.C., shines the spotlight on the relationship between each employee and his or her immediate supervisor. The stronger this relationship, the stronger will be the bond between the worker and the organization. To keep people on-board, all people in management and supervisory positions must understand how to build and maintain positive relationships with their people.

Some employees actually join companies for the opportunity to work with leaders who are known in the field. These employees may or may not work directly for these "gurus," but they're still part of the same team. There is value in continuing the public relations effort on behalf of high-profile achievers in your employ. They can be magnets, attracting other people you'd like to choose to work with your organization.

People want to work for leaders who know where they're going, why, and how they're going to get there. Forward thinking leaders, especially those who are breaking new ground, can set the tone for an Employer of Choice.

ASSESSMENT

The next step in the process is to engage in serious self-assessment. The evaluation can be done in several ways, all of which can be productive in your analysis. Both external and internal assessments can be valuable in defining where you are today. This benchmarking will be very helpful as you move through the transformation process. It will give you a basis of measurement, a starting point from which to measure progress.

Market research firms typically conduct external assessments. Their interviewers can gather impressions from customers, search firms, business writers, college placement offices, competitors, and prospective employees. The reports resulting from this research will give you an interesting picture of how you, the employer, are perceived by the outside world. Most companies don't often look at themselves this way, so the experience might be enlightening.

People in your organization can do the internal research, or you can call in an outside consultant to assist you. In our work, we've often found that employees in most companies will open up much more to an outsider. Using an outsider for at least part of your internal temperature taking is advised.

There are a number of ways you can collect input from your people. You can use one or all of these methods, based on variables such as your culture, where your people are located, their ability to complete questionnaires (literacy level), and the degree of trust in the organization.

Use Surveys

Surveys—pencil and paper, or electronic, using a web-based response system—can gather information from a large number of people quickly and efficiently. A key concern is the design of the survey instrument itself. Psychometric experts recommend that questions be simple and easy to understand, and that they be

worded positively so people don't have to navigate through dou-
ble-negative questions to figure out what answer they want to give.

We use a BASELINE® instrument that asks respondents to answer on a five-level Lichert scale ranging from "Strongly Agree"
to "Strongly Disagree." The survey asks people to respond on two
dimensions: how they see things are now, and how they'd like to
see them. When they answer the should be question, they're indi-
cating their desires and their preferences. When these answers are
compared with current perceptions using gap analysis, the results
can be very telling. The information gathered is extremely useful
in the design of solutions and the development of strategies and
tactics for forward movement. Information is available from The
Herman Group, www.herman.net.

Organize Focus Groups

Focus groups provide opportunities for more keyed-in and more
in-depth discussion. The key here is a good facilitator. Someone
who is skilled at stimulating discussion, in getting people to open
up, and in listening carefully to what is being said can bring out a
tremendous volume of valuable information and insight.

Participants can be picked at random from throughout the organization, or they can come from one particular department. You
can select a representative sample of employees to engage in the
focus group experience, or you can involve everyone. Care should
be taken in the composition of the groups to support open communication. Sometimes people are intimidated by the presence of
their boss, or *any* boss.

Conduct Interviews

Individual interviews can be very fruitful, with one-on-one inter-
changes opening vital issues to more intense exploration. Again,
a skillful interviewer can be much more productive, so select interviewers carefully. A random selection of employees can be a
smart way to go, but you may also want to target certain people
who are in a better position to see what you're looking for. In
many organizations, there are people who should not be left out of

this kind of a process because of what they can contribute, their point of view, or political issues about who is interviewed and who is not.

Review Internal Records

A review of records can produce valuable statistics that may shed light on trends or problem areas. A study of absenteeism by department, for instance, may uncover numbers that might indicate a problem. High absenteeism in a particular department might suggest that there is some sort of motivation problem—people just would rather not come to work for the supervisor of the department. A study of employee tenure may reveal that most of the positions are filled by people who have been with the company for a long period of time. The turnover may be happening in just a few positions and may not be as serious as it seems. A different and more focused strategy would be called for in this instance, rather than a major corporate-wide initiative.

Take a Step Back

It can often be beneficial simply to stop and look at your own organization for a moment. How do things look? Are people happy and productive? Is employee retention high? Do applicants seek opportunities with you, or do you have to invest a large amount of resources in recruiting? How's your employee morale? What do your employee attitude surveys tell you? Have you seen changes in responses over the past few administrations of the surveys?

If all the signals are great, that's good news. If the signals indicate you have some work to do, that's okay, too. Sometimes the process of becoming an Employer of Choice is much more fun than simply confirming that you've already arrived.

Read the Book

We apologize if this strategy seems self-serving, but there's no better way to put it. Read this book. You might also want to read our previous book, *Lean & Meaningful: A New Culture for Corporate America.* Why? These books are loaded with information and advice about trends, strategies, ideas, and methods for creating, building, and sustaining the kind of organization described as an Employer of Choice. We've deliberately included all sorts of examples to stimulate your thinking and to give you an opportunity to measure yourself against other employers and what they're doing.

One of our challenges as authors in this rapidly-emerging field is that we learn about more things we can share—right after the book goes to print. As we continue to gain new insights, we'll share them at www.employerofchoice.net and www.leanandmeaningful.com. Visit us frequently to catch some new ideas.

SELL EMPLOYEES ON THE CONCEPT

The next aspect of your early work in becoming an Employer of Choice is to get the message across to your employees. Using proven marketing strategies to reach your people, a process we call *internal marketing*, sell your people on the value of becoming an Employer of Choice. The sale of the idea probably won't be that difficult; it will be welcome news. The challenge will be in convincing them that you'll actually do it. Remember, actions speak louder than words.

Particularly during the initial transformation phase, it will be important to stay close to your people. Human resource professionals can help monitor how people feel about what's happening, and front-line supervisors will be able to produce valuable feedback.

To emphasize how real this commitment is, senior executives need to be visible and interact with all employees. Their physical connection must be more than just a wave from afar. Now is the time for these executives to engage people in conversation—about the Employer of Choice project and anything else the employees might want to chat about. Skip-level meetings, tours, and

> Dr. John Sullivan, Department Head and Professor of Human Resources at the College of Business at San Francisco State University, recommends engaging an outside consultant to coach you in what to do to become an Employer of Choice or get on the lists of best employers. We salute his work in the field of employee retention. As Certified Management Consultants, we'll be happy to help, but we'll also be the first to warn against rushing out to hire a consultant as a panacea. The important work must be done inside the organization, not by outside consultants.

sitting in on team meetings will all be valuable experiences for senior and mid-level executives. They'll get closer to the people and will probably find ways they can improve or simplify what their people are doing, just by offering a different perspective, clearing a red-tape blockage, or helping to streamline a process.

When people see that things are actually working better, they'll choose to stay—and, very importantly, they will choose to become more a part of the solution than a part of the problem.

BRINGING 'EM IN

As part of the shift to becoming an Employer of Choice, it's wise to tighten the hiring process. *No more hiring "warm bodies."* Insist on hiring only people who will fit with the company culture, who want to choose you as their employer for good reasons, and who will stay with you for a long period of time. Stop the revolving door by becoming more discriminating.

Using pre-employment testing to select the right people for the job can reduce risk, save a lot of time, and facilitate the hiring process. We recommend an instrument known as CheckStart, available through www.checkstart.com. The more selective you are, the greater your chances will be of hiring just the right people. It makes no sense to invest resources to keep people who don't fit. Employers of Choice are populated by employees who fit and who *want* to be there.

The orientation process for new employees may need to be expanded. Employers of Choice offer extensive orientation programs that enable new hires to learn all sorts of valuable things about the employer. Included in enhanced orientations are visits with top executives and briefings on the employer's industry. The best orientations include a comprehensive tour of the facilities with explanations of what happens in each department, in-depth knowledge sharing in the new hire's host department, and information about interdepartmental relationships.

RECOGNITION

When you do good things, it's nice to be recognized for them— whether as an individual or as an employer. Recognition is certainly important in an Employer of Choice environment; it's also important for the employer in a competitive labor market.

As this book goes to press, we are in the final design phase of an international program to recognize employers worthy of being called Employers of Choice. Those employers interested in applying for recognition are welcome to call us at (336) 282-9370 or visit us at www.employerofchoice.net.

This program is not a competitive process that selects the Top 100 or the top whatever. If an employer is worthy of recognition, the recognition will come. There are no limitations on how many employers will be recognized.

Displaying the Employer of Choice plaque will be a source of pride for everyone who works for you. People considering employment with you will certainly take notice. Those who find you on our web site will be inspired to apply, and chances are they'll be the kind of people you're looking for.

We look forward to *your organization* becoming an Employer of Choice.

Notes
1. *The Straits Times*, Singapore, December 13, 1999.
2. *Het Financieele Dagblad*, December 3, 1999.

Appendix A

If You Don't Measure, You Don't Really Know

B usiness leaders like to think that they know intuitively what's going right in their companies—and what's not. However, diagnosis or measurement of the current reality often indicates that their intuitions are not accurate. The first step to truly understanding what's happening in your company is to measure a given situation, then develop information that is as accurate and complete as possible. To obtain accurate and complete information, involve the right people and use the right tools. Ideally, the right tools will quickly and accurately gather information from all the people who have a stake in the company's success.

Most companies know how to assess the financial indicators, but what about measuring the company's performance in the areas that *lead* to improved financial results? There are a number of aspects of organizational operations that contribute—directly or indirectly—to bottom-line results. These indicators also influence how attractive the employer is to current and future employees.

Example of business practices that relate to becoming an Employer of Choice are listed below. Beneath each example are statements about desired conditions to consider as you begin this measurement process.

Teamwork and Accountability
- Teamwork is recognized and rewarded, at our company.
- Holding people accountable for their work is acceptable and encouraged in our company.

Guiding Principles and Values

- Our company has a stated set of values or guiding principles.
- Our employees display honesty, integrity, and ethical conduct.

Leadership Performance

- I feel good about the future of our company, because I have confidence in the vision of our leaders.
- The leadership of our company effectively listens to employees.

Management

- Immediate managers or supervisors care about employees as people.
- Immediate managers or supervisors work with employees on their personal development.
- People feel empowered to manage themselves without close supervision.

Customer Focus

- Customer feedback and satisfaction scores are openly and regularly shared in our company.
- Employees understand how their job adds value to our customers.
- People view co-workers as "internal customers."

Feedback and Engagement

- Employees are encouraged to recommend changes in how work is performed.
- Employees are willing to express their views on issues important to them, even when they know that others may disagree.
- Feedback is acted upon when employees make suggestions for improvement.

Organizational Climate and Employee Loyalty

- Employees feel that working for this company is a great career opportunity.

- Employees' work is challenging and gives them a sense of accomplishment.
- This company is the kind of place people *want* to be—they look forward to coming to work.

Human Resources and Organizational Development
- Employees have input in setting their performance goals.
- Our company successfully hires and retains quality people.
- Marginal performers are expected to meet standards or leave.

Ownership Thinking
- Most employees at our company believe that the hard work they invest today will pay off for them in the future.
- When our company's financial results improve, employees benefit financially.
- Workers watch for ways to strengthen the company's performance.

Business Literacy
- Most employees at our company understand how their actions affect our company's financial results.
- The key numbers that employees directly impact are updated and shared on a regular basis.
- People make an effort to influence results.

These and other key business practices and attitudes must be measured and assessed as part of the process to win long-term success—to be truly recognized as an Employer of Choice.

The idea that we systematically measure what is happening in our organizations seems obvious; however, support for this concept goes beyond intuition and anecdote. In fact, the strong positive relationship between the use of performance measurement/feedback and productivity is one of the most venerable and well-confirmed concepts in applied psychology. A cross section of the empirical studies published in academic literature affirms the positive correlation between the use of measurement/feedback and productivity.[1]

THINGS THAT GET MEASURED GET DONE

We've all heard this mantra. Don't just shut down when you hear it, though; it's true. Today, business throughout the world is on the verge of a quantum shift in the way knowledge is transferred. Increasingly, business leaders want high-value, high-impact, cost-effective solutions in record time. Such dramatic changes have created new knowledge needs for leaders, managers, and employees. Measurements become vitally important in this kind of environment.

The trend toward complexity increases risks associated with business decisions, making it even more important to have a sound information base. Increased complexity means there are more variables to consider. Each of these factors requires leaders to have more and better information on which to base their decisions. Lack of information and measurement in these areas often leads to indecision or wrong decisions, resulting in important issues being left unchanged or even worse, consciously ignored.

An effective assessment process that measures performance and builds commitment throughout the organization is therefore crucial for leaders who drive change in their companies. Most companies have inadequate measurement systems and fail to recognize the importance of implementing an effective assessment process. They're not getting the information they need. Consequently, there is a lack of commitment, direction, and drive for continuous improvement throughout the organization. The areas of opportunity are not obvious.

An effective assessment is one that can be repeated in the future and one that determines both now and later if progress has been made. If a first assessment provides the diagnosis and prescribed change initiatives, then re-assessments provide the necessary check-ups. Continuous assessment ensures not only that goals are developed, but also that improvements are actually taking place and better results are achieved. Whenever new goals are established, a corresponding measurement system should be established to track their performance.

In summary, the best companies establish an effective system to regularly measure and re-measure their performance in key business practices. The information allows them to make course corrections that drive continuous improvement efforts, and speed up the rate at which improvements occur. Employees recognize even more fully the importance of their jobs, and performance improves. *Things that get measured get done.*

THE NUTS AND BOLTS

Performance measurement can be a complicated process. However, academic studies support the proposition that the identification, measurement, and thoughtful utilization of important organizational metrics is associated with productivity and desired outcomes for those organizations which use the process effectively.[2] In a 1999 article in the *Journal of Business Strategy*, David Hofrichter suggests that competitive advantage is achieved by being able to align performance measurement processes with an organizational culture that is appropriate for the operating environment.[3] He points to General Electric, McDonald's, Wal-Mart, and Federal Express as prime examples of companies which have achieved a competitive advantage by linking performance measurement with the establishment of cultures that more consistently shaped the behaviors of their people as compared to their competitors.

In the area of Human Resource Management (HRM), academics tend to differentiate between two forms of endeavor and effort—tactical and strategic. Tactical HRM activities involve such traditional functions as recruitment, selection, training, legal compliance, and compensation. Strategic HRM involves more recently developed innovations such as empowering employees, improving communication, creative benefit offerings, and self-directed work teams. The day-to-day maintenance of the business is guided by its tactical HRM activities, whereas strategic HRM activities are concerned more with innovation as a means of gaining competitive advantage. The only study to investigate the relative contribution of the measurement of each of these two types of HRM practices found that strategic HRM activities, not tactical ones, contributed significantly to firm financial performance and employee productivity.[4]

In 1995, GE began an initiative rooted in measurement called Six Sigma. Six Sigma is a statistical measurement tool for measuring the quality of products and services. A level of Six Sigma represents the best of quality with the virtual elimination of defects from every product and process in a company (no more than 3.4 defects per million). A measurement system such as Six Sigma does more than just "keep score."[5] *It provides a clear line of sight from where the organization is to where it wants to go. It provides a common language throughout the organization that enables people to share ideas and continuously find ways to improve.*

General Electric, one of the world's largest and most profitable organizations, makes change happen at unparalleled speeds. Demonstration of best business practices is seen throughout their organization in everything from their leadership-development system to their "QMI—Quick Market Intelligence" meetings, which they developed from similar practices at Wal-Mart.

Setting a goal of virtually no defects is exciting, but actually putting a measurement system in place to track performance represents commitment. This level of commitment in improving their business practices has made GE the leader it is today.

The Most Important Business Practices

A number of companies specializing in measurement and research have explored the relationship of various performance indicators to bottom line results. Those results can be financial achievements, or in our case, workforce stability and productivity. We asked the measurement professionals at Success Profiles in Bozeman, Montana, for their perspective and experience.

Leadership Performance and Feedback and Engagement

They found above average scores in both Leadership Performance and Feedback and Engagement to be the most important business practices when it comes to organizational growth in revenue. In a study of 150 organizations, Success Profiles compared organizational growth rates to leadership scores and feedback and engagement scores. They found a high correlation between companies performing well in these two business practices and growth in revenue. In practice, the companies who scored high in feedback and engagement experienced above 50% growth in revenue per year!

Leadership is fairly universally defined, but what is feedback and engagement? If communication is information going down and across in an organization, feedback is what is going up—the concept of listening to and actually doing something about what employees are saying. Engagement is the degree to which people are involved in the decision-making process in a business. A business excelling in feedback and engagement inspires employees, because their feedback is elicited, valued, and acted on. They really feel like a part of the flow, the "heartbeat" of the organization.

Teamwork Contributes Less

Other business practices, such as teamwork, don't seem to have the same result on revenue, according to the work performed by Success Profiles. Organizations must have teamwork, but any more than a little does not seem to contribute to rapid growth. Studies found that as scores increased above the average level for teamwork, the impact on revenue growth was minimal. This finding reinforces our emphasis that one-on-one relationships are supplanting team relationships in achieving business results.

Soliciting and Responding to Feedback

In every aspect of business, you must listen to your employees' perceptions, or you won't know your company very well. Without feedback from your employees, the best you can do is guess. When there isn't a steady flow of information up to the leadership from the employees, decisions are made without all the necessary facts. Don't miss the wealth of untapped intelligence available to you. Ask your people for their feedback in ongoing conversations, meetings and through surveys.

Remember, though, that once you have asked for feedback and engaged employees in the process, you have essentially "let the

Relationship Between Teamwork Scores and Growth in Revenue

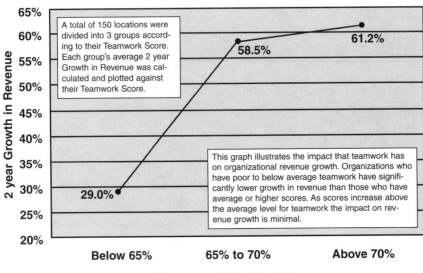

A total of 150 locations were divided into 3 groups according to their Teamwork Score. Each group's average 2 year Growth in Revenue was calculated and plotted against their Teamwork Score.

58.5%

61.2%

29.0%

This graph illustrates the impact that teamwork has on organizational revenue growth. Organizations who have poor to below average teamwork have significantly lower growth in revenue than those who have average or higher scores. As scores increase above the average level for teamwork the impact on revenue growth is minimal.

Below 65% 65% to 70% Above 70%

Teamwork Index Score

genie out of the bottle." Expectations of follow-through are now raised, and the desire to see feedback put to action is increased. A company that is not committed to following through is better off never initiating the feedback and engagement process. Asking for employees' opinions and then failing to address and act on them will have a negative impact, resulting in reduced employee morale and satisfaction.

The Benefits of Measurement

Creating change in an organization is often a difficult and seemingly insurmountable challenge. A proven way to insure a successful initiative is to commit to an effective measurement system and implementation of a plan to handle the exposed opportunities for improvement. A properly designed and implemented system will provide these benefits to any change initiative:

- Create a high level of commitment throughout the organization
- Provide practical and straight forward feedback

The Contrast between Feedback and Engagement Scores and Leadership Scores and their Relationship to Growth in Revenue

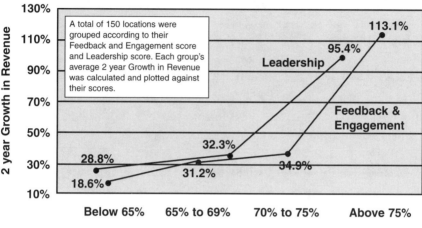

Business Practices Appraisal Index Score

- Establish reliable and repeatable baseline performance measures to determine improvements
- Create "Actionable Knowledge" that prioritizes key business issues
- Provide a comparison of your company's performance to the "best of the best" (benchmarking with top-performing companies)
- Create organizational alignment on the key issues of the business
- Identify perception gaps between senior leadership, management, and employees
- Serve as a motivating road map by creating a clear line of sight so that employees see the relationship their work has on business success
- Identify the real drivers of employee retention and financial performance
- Build a business case for change and improvement with links to financial results

- Become integrated with the company's action planning to continually drive change
- Validate the choices people make—to join an organization, become engaged in its work, and to stay for an extended period of time.

WHAT EMPLOYERS OF CHOICE MEASURE

Now that you have an overview of what measurement is and can be, and how to use it, we'll discuss in more detail how to implement measurement systems in your company.

The Five Dashboard Indicators

There seems to be a lack of universal measures or standards beyond basic financial accounting for measuring business performance. From its research, Success Profiles has identified a set of universal business performance measures ("dashboard indicators"):

Business Practices—leadership and management
Business Processes—operational and efficiency measures
Employee Measures—employee satisfaction, development, and retention
Customer/Stakeholder Measures—customer satisfaction and loyalty
Financial Results—financial ratios, profitability, and growth rates

For a company to measure its success with a balanced approach, its leaders must focus on and measure each of the above criteria. Each one is important in developing the kind of organization for which people want to work.

Measure What's Most Important

It is essential that companies track both hard and soft measurements. Hard measures are quantitative measurements that provide objective results that can be used to evaluate performance and trends over time. These quantitative categories may include financial outcomes, turnover rates, application rates, income statements, and balance sheets.

Soft measurements include attitudes, feelings, and perceptions. These allow companies to identify the major issues (both positive and negative) affecting them, by utilizing subjective feedback. These measurements reveal gaps in perception between stakeholders; track employee morale and organizational climate; and establish baseline performance measures that are used to align perceptions.

The Cause and Effect Relationship

By combining both soft and hard measurements, companies can establish which non-financial measures will most affect their overall financial performance. This process, known as Integrated Performance Measurement, acts as a catalyst for organizational change efforts by providing relevant, precise, useful, timely, and creditable feedback to an organization.

In the past, many firms disregarded soft data, such as customer and employee attitudes and satisfaction, because they did not know how it could be quantified. In just the past decade, companies have begun to integrate the different measurement components into one comprehensive system. Today, prominent companies such as Levi Strauss and Co., Sears, and Toyota are using state-of-the-art business performance measurement systems to incorporate soft data.

Measurement is often difficult. "Unlike revenues and profits, soft data [such as customer and employee attitudes or satisfaction and/or retention] are hard to define and collect."[6] Because many companies have not invested the time,

Sears, Roebuck and Co. knows. Through ongoing data collection, analysis, modeling, and experimentation, they have developed what they call Total Performance Indicators (TPI). Sears understands the layers of factors that drive employee attitudes. They know that employee attitudes have a domino effect on the retention, satisfaction, and financials of all their stakeholders.

Sears, known for its radical strategic turnaround and dramatic improvements in financial results, suggests that there is a distinct chain of cause and effect linking—from employee behavior to customer behavior to increased profits. Furthermore, because Sears found that behavior depends primarily on attitude, attitude became its the focal point.

energy, or resources to measure business culture effectively, how then can they quantifiably know how employees and customers relate to the end profit?

CEO Arthur Martinez and a group of more than 100 top-level executives spent approximately 3 years rebuilding the company around its customers. Sears found that implementation of an employee-customer-profit chain was not easy. The transformation required a change in logic and overall business culture.

Finding the right measurement systems that will combine soft and hard data can be a lengthy task, but it will more than pay for itself. Search for ways to incorporate both soft and hard data and the measurement of that data into your everyday business practices and decisions.

EMPLOYER OF CHOICE RECOGNITION

Every organization—corporations, government agencies, not-for-profits—including yours, has an opportunity to participate in the Employer of Choice (EoC) Recognition Program. The program was designed with many benefits in mind. It promotes the use of measurement and benchmarking to facilitate the steady improvement within a company; it also gives well-deserved recognition to truly worthy employers. The following sections outline the award program. For further details and application information contact The Herman Group at www.herman.net or at (336) 282-9370 or visit www.employer ofchoice.net.

Application Process

The application process is the first step for a company in being recognized as an Employer of Choice. Although this is a complete and thorough evaluation of your organization, we have emphasized *simplicity* in the design of the process for the recognition program. The process has been streamlined to require limited documentation and paperwork from the applying organization.

During the application process, the applicant selects an internal champion. The champion is likely to be in a leadership position within the human resources department. He or she must have a comprehensive understanding of the organization's business practices or access to the people who do. The champion submits an application that contains an evaluation of the company's performance in each of the Employer of Choice criteria (listed earlier in the book and on the application), discussion and documentation of how each of the criteria is met in the company, and applicable performance data (financial and human resource). This information is used to establish the foundation for the formal assessment process. An independent oversight panel will review the organization's application to ensure fairness and consistency.

Employer Input

Who is better to evaluate a company as a potential Employer of Choice than the employees? Success Profiles, an independent measurement firm, will conduct the formal assessment process. This firm has measured the business practices of hundreds of companies around the world. In collaboration with Success Profiles' researchers, we have designed a formal assessment process to gather feedback from at least 80% of the employees, supervisors, managers, and leaders of applying organizations.

The EoC assessment tool is a valid, reliable, and anonymous instrument containing a number of statements to which employees will respond. Administration is a simple process, best performed in a facilitated setting, and takes approximately 20 minutes to complete. Success Profiles designed the process to require minimal effort on the part of the applying organization.

The reports will be generated from the employee responses and will provide a comprehensive assessment of the how the company is performing in relation to the Employer of Choice criteria. The reports will display perception gaps, strengths, areas needing improvement, and comparisons to normative data collected from numerous other organizations. They will also reveal where the company is excelling and where it has opportunities for improvement. The information represented in the reports provides the foundation for successful change initiatives in the organization.

Results of the employee survey will be provided to each applying company for its own use in strengthening vital aspects of the EoC criteria.

Scoring Process and Recognition

The Employer of Choice recognition process utilizes the application and formal assessment to score each applying company. The company will receive a score for each of the measured criteria as well as an overall score. These scores are then compared against an index score to determine if an organization should receive recognition in any of the stated criteria. Companies that demonstrate outstanding results in all measured areas will earn the designation of "Employer of Choice." The information from the Employer of Choice companies is then submitted to an independent expert panel to confirm our Employer of Choice selections. Employers of Choice will be recognized publicly, with press releases, presentation of a plaque for display, and recognition on the www.employerofchoice.net Web site.

Why Apply?

Companies should apply for the Employer of Choice Award for several reasons. It is not a competition, but an investment in your organization's future success. The company will learn how the Employer of Choice criteria apply to its culture and will receive a template that evaluates its current and future state; the real value is in the discovery process itself. By making the Employer of Choice designation a common goal, you will encourage corporate introspection and provide unparalleled opportunities for better understanding the employees, procedures, and culture of your company. Striving to become an Employer of Choice fosters positive change throughout the organization. Your results will be provided along with data from (other) world-class organizations, so that you will have the opportunity to compare and learn from them.

WHAT NEXT

Whether you are measuring your eligibility for the Employer of Choice recognition or conducting some other evaluation of your performance, it's important to explore uses of the information you gather. Obviously, using the data to guide internal improvements is expected. Why measure something if you're not going to use the results to evaluate and improve what you're doing?

External comparisons can be as valuable, if not more valuable, than comparisons of periodic results of internal studies. How does your organization compare to others? What can you learn from the experience and achievement of other employers? The external comparison process, known as benchmarking, gives you an opportunity to measure your results against similar results from high performing organizations. How do you stand up to the companies you'd like to emulate? What could you do differently that would make a difference for your organization?

When benchmarking, a company does not necessarily need to use intra-industry comparisons. After L.L. Bean demonstrated excellence in the area of warehouse operations, for instance, Xerox took advantage of an opportunity to examine L.L. Bean operations firsthand and apply what they learned. The fact that one organization's product is clothing and the other's is office equipment did not matter. Once recognized, excellence in most functions can be adapted and modeled throughout varying organizations. What works in other companies may well make a difference in yours.

MEASUREMENT TO IMPLEMENTATION

Change is never easy for anyone or any organization. It takes courage. It's human nature to feel uncomfortable with anything new. It is natural to put up barriers to sources of potential discomfort. This hesitancy to change is why the way an organization proceeds at this point is critical to the success of the change effort.

To be effective, companies must review the results of the assessment—*whether from application for EoC recognition or otherwise*—in detail, and share them with employees, management, and other stakeholders immediately. It is important to note, however, that no matter how eager an organization is to make change happen, it must be ready to do so organizationally. Organizational readiness can be measured using the following framework:

- A clear vision or line of sight as to where an organization is headed
- People who have the skills to do work differently
- Incentives (ownership, bonuses) which provide motivation for change
- Resources (money, tools and people) that are available to be successful
- An action plan which details the step-by-step process for change exists

If any one of these criteria is missing, one or all of the following results will occur:

When people have the skills to do their jobs differently, the incentives in place to motivate change, adequate resources are available, a detailed action plan exists, *but no vision* of where the organization is headed, the result will most likely be *confusion* and *failure*.

When people can see where the organization is headed, the incentives are in place to motivate change, adequate resources are available, and a detailed action plan exists, *but employees lack the skills* to do their jobs differently, the result will most likely be *anxiety*.

When people can see where the organization is headed, have the skills to do their jobs differently, adequate resources are available, and a detailed action plan exists, *without the incentives in place* to motivate change, the result will most likely be change that is *too gradual*.

When people can see where the organization is headed, have the skills to do their jobs differently, the incentives in place to motivate change, a detailed action plan exists, *but lack the resources* needed, the result will most likely be *frustration*.

When people have a vision of where the organization is headed, the skills to do their jobs differently, the incentives in place to motivate change, and adequate resources are available, *but don't have a detailed action plan,* the result will most likely be *false starts.*

Corporate leaders must analyze the business practices, processes, policies and procedures, attitudes, and behaviors that are contributing to their "as is" state, to determine which improvements need to be made. Performance gaps between the "as is" and the "desired" state should then be reviewed to develop an action plan.

To ensure the success of the initiative, specific, hard-target milestones (timetables) with a structured approach that includes purpose and objectives, goals, strategies, tactics, and resources required should be established.

Companies must continuously manage change. This means executing on the initiatives developed and re-measuring at specific intervals (2 to 4 times per year) to determine if improvement efforts have been successful.

Getting Started: Converting Information and Ideas into Action

When it comes to improving your business, it can be a challenge to know where to begin. It's unrealistic to think that you can do it all at once. *You must prioritize.* You must identify the areas that will provide the greatest benefit for your effort—your employees are a great place to start. Measuring your employees' perceptions and attitudes is often the first step in organization-wide improvement. People are the key to organizational performance. Building a happy, stable, productive workforce of people who *want* to be there makes a tremendous difference.

Use Outside Help for Objectivity

If you are going to invest the time and resources into an improvement effort or change initiative, ask yourself, "Am I basing my decisions on sound data?" Use a reputable outside firm that will ensure accurate and timely measurement. The benefit of using an outside firm is the assurance that employees' responses will remain anonymous. In addition, a firm that specializes in measurement should have statistically sound instruments and normative data to enable you to benchmark your performance against other organizations.

Using the services of an outside consultant can help you evaluate at your efforts and your results more objectively. Professional consultants can ask questions and raise issues that may be politically uncomfortable for people inside the organization. As Certified Management Consultants, we encourage you to engage consultants who are certified or at least members of The Institute of Management Consultants (IMC).

Make a Commitment to Follow Through

Once you ask the questions, there is no going back. When company leaders open themselves to feedback, they have an obligation to respond. Possibly the most constructive thing corporate leaders can do is to ask stakeholders for feedback; possibly the most destructive thing they can do is to not act on it. Within one month of soliciting feedback, leaders should thank the respondents for their feedback, summarize what they learned, and tell the respondents how the company is planning to use the feedback.

Throughout this book, we have indicated that employees be kept informed about business practices. Now we urge you to keep them informed about changes you will be implementing as you work through the measurement process.

Be Recognized As An Employer Of Choice

Becoming an Employer of Choice is not an easy feat. It requires a commitment from your organization to continually strive towards ever-improved business practices. Accurate and valuable measurement tactics are just one element of this process. The recognition as an "Employer of Choice" has benefits well beyond bragging rights, but with it comes the responsibility to maintain heightened standards. Take the Employer of Choice challenge, and propel your company to new heights.

Contributions to this appendix were provided in part by Tom Olivo, Donna Wallace, Justin Martin, Darcee Richmond, and Annah Moore of Success Profiles, and Dr. Bill Brown of Montana State University.

Notes

1. Increased productivity and decreased absenteeism among blue collar telephone company employees (Kim, J.S., & Hammer, W. C., "Effect of performance feedback and goal setting on productivity and satisfaction in and organizational setting," *Journal of Applied Psychology*, 1976); increased courtesy behavior among service personnel (Johnson, M. D., & Fawcett, S. B., "Courteous service: Its assessment and modification in a human service organization," *Journal of Applied Behavior Analysis*, 1994); reduced machine set-up times (Wittkopp, C. J., Rowan, J. F., & Poling, A. "Use of a feedback package to reduce machine set-up time in a manufacturing setting," *Journal of Organizational Behavior Management*, February, 1990); productivity of a university admissions office (Wilk, L. A., & Redmon, W. K., "A daily adjusted goal setting and feedback procedure for improving productivity in a university admissions department," *Journal of Organizational Behavior Management*, February, 1990); productivity in a manufacturing setting (Gowen, C. R. III, & Jennings, S. A., "The effects of changes in participation and group size on gainsharing success: A case study" *Journal of Organizational Behavior Management*, February, 1990); innovations in a public utilities company (Smith, J. M., Kaminski, B. J., & Wylie, R. G. (1990), "May I make a suggestion?: Corporate support for innovation. *Journal of Organizational Behavior Management, November*, 1990), wait staff productivity (George, J., & Hopkins, B. L. "Effects of performance-contingent pay for waitpersons," *Journal of Applied Behavior Analysis*, December, 1989); number of quality inspections performed in the public sector (Nordstrum, R., Hall, R. V., Lorenzi, P., & Delquadri, J., "Organizational behavior modification in the public sector: Three field experiments," *Journal of Organizational Behavior Management*, September, 1988); productivity in a military setting, (Pritchard, R. D., Jones, S. D., Roth, P. L., Stuebing, K. K., & Ekeberg, S. E., "Effects of group feedback, goal setting, and incentives on organizational productivity," *Journal of Applied Psychology*, July, 1988); and billed hours per day for mechanics (Evans, K. M., Kienast, P., & Mitchell, T. R. (1988). The effects of lottery incentive programs on performance. *Journal of Organizational Behavior Management*, September, 1988).

2. Waldman, D.A., and Atwater, L..E, *The Power of 360 Degree Feedback: How to Leverage Performance Evaluation for Top Productivity* (Houston: Gulf Publishing, 1998).

3. Hofrichter, D.A.. "Secrets of the rich and famous," *The Journal of Business Strategy*, July/August, 1999.
4. Huselid, M. A., Jackson, S. E., and Schuler, R. A., "Technical and Strategic Human Resource Management Effectiveness as Determinants of Firm Performance," *Academy of Management Journal* 40 (1997).
5. Hal Clifford, "Six Sigma," *Continental*, November, 1997.
6. Ricci, Anthony J., Kirn, Steven P., and Quinn, Richard T., "The Employee-Customer-Profit Chain at Sears," *Harvard Business Review* (January–February 1998.

RECOMMENDED BOOKS

Alessandra, Tony. *Charisma: Seven Steps to Developing the Magnetism that Leads to Success.*

Case, John. *Open Book Management: The Coming Business Revolution.*

Edelston, Martin and Marion Buhagier. *I-Power.*

Fyock, Catherine D. *America's Work Force is Coming of Age: What Every Business Needs to Know to Recruit, Train, Manage, and Retain an Aging Work Force.*

Fyock, Catherine D. *Get the Best: How to Recruit the People You Want.*

Fyock, Catherine D. *UnRetirement: A Career Guide for the Retired . . . the Soon-to-Be-Retired . . . the Never-to-Be-Retired.*

Hanson, Dan. *Cultivating Common Ground: Releasing the Power of Relationships at Work.*

Hanson, Dan. *A Place to Shine: Emerging from the Shadows at Work.*

Herman, Roger. *Keeping Good People: Strategies for the #1 Problem Facing Business Today.*

Herman, Roger. *The Process of Excelling.*

Herman, Roger. *Signs of the Times.*

Herman, Roger and Joyce Gioia. *Lean & Meaningful: A New Culture for Corporate America.*

Judy, Richard W. and Carol D'Amico. *Workforce 2020.*

McCoy, Thomas J. *Creating an Open Book Organization.*

Nelson, Bob. *1001 Ways to Energize Employees.*

Nelson, Bob. *1001 Ways to Reward Employees.*

Nelson, Bob. *1001 Ways to Take Initiative at Work.*

Outlaw, Wayne. *Smart Staffing.*

Reichheld, Frederick F. *The Loyalty Effect: The Hidden Force Behind Growth, Profits, and Lasting Value.*

Russell, Chuck. *Right Person, Right Job.*

Senge, Peter. *The Fifth Discipline.*

Senge, Peter. *The Fifth Discipline Fieldbook.*

Slutsky, Jeff. *Streetfighting.*

Stack, Jack. *The Great Game of Business.*

Vleck, Jr., Donald J. and Jeffrey P. Davidson. *The Domino Effect.*

Yerkes, Leslie. *301 Ways to Have Fun at Work.*

RESOURCE LIST

American Society for Training & Development
  1640 King Street, Box 1443
  Alexandria, Virginia 22313-2043
  703-683-8100
  www.astd.com

BASELINE® Surveys
  The Herman Group
  3400 Willow Grove Court
  Greensboro, North Carolina 27410
  (336) 282-9370
  www.herman.net

CEO America, the Children's Educational Opportunity Foundation, helps provide low-income parents with opportunity scholarships—giving them a choice as to where their children attend elementary and secondary schools. For more information, visit www.ceoamerica.org.

Charities@Work is another option for charities to support. United Way America's Charities, Earth Share, Combined Health Appeal, and International Service Agencies together are known as Charities@Work.

"CheckStart" applicant screening instrument. Available through www.checkstart.com

ChildrenFirst *www.childrenfirst.com*

Coach University
  Post Office Box 881595
  Steamboat Springs, Colorado 80488-1595
  (800) 48-COACH
  www.coachu.com

Employee Services Management Association
2211 York Road, Suite 207
Oakbrook, Illinois 60523
(630) 368-1280
www.esmassn.org

Habitat for Humanity *www.habitat.org*

Junior Achievement *www.ja.org*

Mentor U
311 Fourth Avenue, Suite 611
San Diego, California 92101
(619) 615-0800
www.mentoru.com/herman

Muzak: *www.muzak.com*

National Safety Council
1121 Spring Lake Drive
Itasca, Illinois 60143
630-775-2231
www.nsc.org

Open Forum List-Serve operated by the Workforce Stability Institute. Subscribe at the web site: *www.employee.org*

Operation Smile *www.operationsmile.org*

Pet Assure *www.petassure.com*

Society for Human Resource Management
1800 Duke Street
Alexandria, Virginia 22314-3499
800-283-7476
www.shrm.org

Steelcase (Personal Harbor)

http://www.steelcase.com/products/subcategory.html?subcategory=per sonalharbor&category=systems.

Workforce Stability Institute
  3400 Willow Grove Court
  Greensboro, North Carolina 27410
  (336) 282-1480
  www.employee.org

ORGANIZATIONS CITED IN THIS BOOK

1-800-FLOWERS

3M

ABN Amro

Air Mauritius

Allied Signal

Allstate Insurance

American Automobile Association

American Cancer Society

American Express

American Freightways Corporation

American Management Association

American Red Cross

American Society for Training & Development

America's Charities

Ames Rubber

Arizona Mail Order

Arthur Andersen

Bank Boston

Baptist Hospital, Inc.

Bank of America

Bellcore

Ben & Jerry's, Inc.

Blades & Associates

Blue Cross Blue Shield of Massachusetts

Boddie Noell

The Body Shop

Boston Celtics

Boy Scouts of America

Bright Horizons Family Solutions

Burger King

Brink's Home Security

Burrell Professional Labs

Business & Professional Women

Business Stationery, Inc.

Camet Corporation

Carolina Power & Light

CDW

Central Florida Work and Gain Economic Self-Sufficiency Coalition

Center for Creative Leadership

Central Transport

CEO America

Challenger, Gray, & Christmas

Charities@Work

Cheesecake Factory

Children's Educational Opportunity Foundation

CIGNA Insurance Group

Community College of Philadelphia

Copley, Ohio, High School

Citibank

Combined Health Appeal

Corporate Challenge

Daimler/Chrysler Corporation

DataTel

Dearfield Associates, Inc.

Dell University

Deloitte Touche

Delta Air Lines

Dick Hall Productions

Digital

Disney

Dog-ma

Domino's Pizza

Drexel University

Earth Share

Edelman Group

Ellis Memorial Hospital

Emergency Medical Associates

Emerson Electric

Employment Law Training, Inc.

English & Gloven

Ericsson Corporation

Exchange Clubs

Families & Work Institute

Farm Fresh Bakery

Ford Motor Company

Gallup Organization

General Electric

Girl Scouts of America

Glaxo-Wellcome

Gold's Gym

Goodwill Industries

GTECH Holdings Corporation

Gymboree

Habitat for Humanity

Hall Ambulance Company

Hallmark

HA-LO Industries

Hardee's Restaurants

Henry County-Martinsville United Way

The Herman Group

Herman Miller

IHS HelpDesk Services

Home Depot

Hudson Institute & Walker Information, The

Iams

Ingram Micro

Intel

International Service Agencies

J. P. Morgan

John Hancock Insurance

Johnson & Johnson

Junior Achievement

Justice Telecom

KinderKare

Kiwanis

Land O' Lakes

LaPetite Academy

LensCrafters

Levi Strauss & Company

Littler Mendelson

Lockheed Martin

Lucent Technologies

Malden Mills Industries

Make a Wish Foundation

Manco, Inc.

March of Dimes

Marriott Hotels

Mary Kay Cosmetics

Mastercard

Mastery Works, Inc.

McDonald's Restaurants

McKinsey & Co.

Meals On Wheels

Medtronics

Mentor University

Merck Pharmaceuticals

Meridia Healthcare Systems

Microsoft

Modern International Graphics, Inc.

Morley Builders

Motek

Motorola University

Muzak

National Institute for Literacy

The National Safety Council

National Sleep Foundation

Newell Rubbermaid

New Jersey Department of Labor

Niagara Mohawk

Noble & Associates

Nordstrom

Northern Virginia Regional
   Partnership

Northwest Airlines

Nortel Networks

Operation Smile

Oppenheimer Funds Services

Opryland Hotel

Pan Pacific Hotels

Patrice Tanaka & Company

PC Connection

Pet Assure

Pittsburgh (Pennsylvania) Airport

PricewaterhouseCoopers

Red Cross

Rockwell

Rotary

Ruritan

Ruth's Chris Steak House

San Francisco 49ers

San Francisco State University

Sara Lee Knit Products

SAS Institute

Save the Children

Schwartz Communications

Sears

Sea World

Sertoma

Six Flags

SoftChoice

Southwest Airlines

Springfield Remanufacturing
   Company

Sprint University of Excellence

St. Barnabas Hospital

Stanley Furniture

Steelcase

Successories

SunU

The Taylor Group

Temple University

Texas Instruments

Thomson Corporation, Thomson
University
Time Warner Communications
Trevira Division of Hoeschst
Celanese
United Air Lines
Uni-Mail List Corp
United Healthcare
United Nations International
Children's Emergency Fund
(UNICEF)
United Parcel Service
United States Jaycees
United Way
Universal Studios Escape

University of Delaware
University of Pennsylvania
Unysis
Varian Oncology Systems
Verifone University
VF Corporation
Volvo Truck Corporation
Wal-Mart
Widender University
Warner Lambert
Wilson McHenry Company
Wilton Conner Packaging
World Gym
Xerox Corporation

ABOUT THE AUTHORS

Roger E. Herman

Roger E. Herman is Chief Executive Officer of The Herman Group, a management consulting, speaking, and training firm he founded in 1980.

After serving as a Counterintelligence Special Agent during the Viet Nam era, he held a variety of management and sales positions in manufacturing, retail, distribution, and direct sales. He has also served as a City Manager. A graduate of Hiram College, Roger holds a master's degree from The Ohio State University in the field of Public Administration.

As a sought-after speaker, Roger earned the coveted Certified Speaking Professional (CSP) designation from the National Speakers Association. He is also a Certified Management Consultant (CMC)—one of only 15 people in the world to hold both the CSP and CMC. Roger is a member of the Society for Human Resource Management and the World Future Society.

A Strategic Business Futurist concentrating on workforce and workplace trends, Roger's forecasts are consistently on target and his commentaries about trends are penetrating and provocative.

Roger has published more than 600 articles, writes a column that is carried by a number of trade magazines, and frequently appears on radio and television talk shows. He is Contributing Editor on workforce and workplace trends for *The Futurist* magazine.

As the early advocate and author of *Keeping Good People* (first published in 1990), Roger is known as "the father of employee retention." He is widely recognized for his work in the field of workforce stability. The current edition of his seminal book is the #5 best seller for the Society for Human Resource Management and has been featured by a number of book clubs.

Joyce L. Gioia

Joyce L. Gioia is President of The Herman Group, based in Greensboro, North Carolina. A consultant since 1984, she is recognized as a Certified Management Consultant by the Institute of Management Consultants. A specialist in adding value, Joyce gained a national reputation for her work in direct marketing, product launches, and arranging strategic alliances. At the age of 28, she became the youngest magazine publisher in the country. Recognized as an innovator, she is known for her ability to understand and explain consumerism trends in the United States and in other countries and regions. She intertwines this knowledge with her work in the field of human resources to bring a totally new dimension to workforce stability strategy.

Joyce is a graduate of the University of Denver, Joyce holds a Masters of Business Administration from Fordham University. She also holds a Masters in Theology and a Masters in Counseling from The New Seminary in New York City. She has taught marketing at the university level at several schools.

A frequent speaker for corporate and trade association audiences, Joyce is a Professional Member of the World Future Society and the National Speakers Association. She is also a member of the American Society for Training and Development. A Fellow of the Workforce Stability Institute, Joyce is frequently cited in the news media for her expertise on workforce and workplace trends and internal marketing. She is regularly quoted in publications like *Business Week*, *Entrepreneur*, *Inc.*, and *The Christian Science Monitor*. She has also appeared on many radio and television talk shows and was featured by a cable network as well. Her concentration is communicating messages through organizational cultures to encourage people to remain productively with their employers for longer periods of times.

INDEX